OCDF Publications
is a division of Our Chinese Daughters Foundation (OCDF), a 501c3 non-profit organization, based in Bloomington, IL USA and Beijing, China. OCDF is dedicated to providing high quality culture programs and publications to children, teenagers, parents, and educators. Find us online at www.ocdf.org/publications.

Lead writers
Sherisse Pham
Suí Hóng 隋宏

Editors
Dr. Jane Liedtke
Emily Liedtke
Wesley Smith
Megan Zaroda

Researchers
Bīngmǎ 冰马
David Wáng Yúnhóng 王云洪

Design
Jonathan Tsao
Wáng Lán 王兰
(Chinabeat Ltd.)

Project Manager
Suí Hóng 隋宏

Project Developed By
Dr. Jane Liedtke

ISBN-13: 978-1-934487-54-9
ISBN-10: 1-934487-54-6

Copyright © 2009 by OCDF Publications, a division of Our Chinese Daughters Foundation, Inc.

Maps Copyright © 2007 held by the Chengdu Cartographic Publishing House

Educators are welcome to request from OCDF Publications complimentary teaching support materials that accompany this book. Please email: OCDFPublications@ocdf.org

Although the authors and OCDF Publications have taken all reasonable care in preparing this book, we make no warranty about the accuracy or completeness of its content and, to the maximum extent permitted, disclaim all liability arising from its use.

All rights reserved. No part of this book may be reproduced or transmitted in any form or by any means, electronic or mechanical, including photocopying, recording, or by any information storage and retrieval system, without permission in writing from the Publisher.

Contents

Overview	8		Socioeconomy	16
Jiangsu in Brief			*Economics Chat*	
Resources	10		Capital	20
Nature Notes			*Experiencing Nanjing*	
History	12		People	24
Jiangsu Rewind			*An Oral Portrait*	

Heritage	28		Handy Tools	
The Written World	28		Map of Jiangsu	5
Fine Art	32		Map of Nanjing	6
Kunqu Opera	36		References	62
Science and Technology	38		Acknowledgements	63
Tradition	64			

Special Feature 40
Chinese Gardens

Highlights 50
Destinations 50
Local Flavors 58
Collector's Corner 60

Old lady selling kids' sandals in a water town in southern Jiangsu

Introduction

For the vast majority of Westerners, China has remained a mystery that is centuries old. China is enormous. Coupled with its 5,000-year history of traditions, the country has demonstrated that it is both quick to change, yet slow to relinquish its traditional values. Every year, China continues to attract visitors from all over the world. Some come to crack the riddle of Chinese culture; some are sent on business ventures; still others make the trip for the pure excitement of the place. And, there are those who fall in love with the country and decide to make a life there.

Modern China rests on the fulcrum between fantasy and reality. The growing interest in China, especially among the younger generation, has accelerated to form a "China Wave." Anything China-related is pursued with vigor: the language, the culture, the history, the food, and the people.

As the fascination with China's past, present, and future grows, visitors are exploring every facet of its mosaic of indigenous cultures, languages and customs. Each visitor takes his or her own impressions of the country, leaving the riddle intact. They return home with an open invitation to visit China again and discover anew as China changes.

One summer, Emma, a high school student from Chicago, Illinois in the USA, embarked on a journey to the Far East. Studying Chinese for two years prior to her departure, she had become passionate about anything and everything Chinese. As part of an exchange program, she was set to make a whirlwind summer tour of eastern China, particularly Ānhuī 安徽, Shànghǎi 上海, Shāndōng 山东, Zhèjiāng 浙江, Jiāngsū 江苏, Jiāngxī 江西, and Fújiàn 福建 provinces.

Jiāngsū was a fascinating province that Emma toured. She walked the water towns of Zhōuzhuāng 周庄, Tónglǐ 同里, and Lùzhí 甪直, explored the exquisite gardens in Sūzhōu 苏州, and sailed on the picturesque Tàihú 太湖 (Lake Tài 太). In due course, Emma broadened her cultural understanding by meeting locals and learning about the history of Nánjīng 南京. The visit to Huáxī 华西, the wealthiest Chinese village, has also given Emma some ideas of the economic reforms that have made Jiāngsū (and the whole country) the place it is today.

Let's embark on this wonderful journey with Emma and see where her experiences lead her.

Explore-A-Province in China®

Legend 图例

政区图图例
Administrative Map Legend

★ 北京 Beijing	首都 Capital	特别行政区界 Special administrative zone boundary		1256	高程注记 Elevation in metres
◎ 南京 Nanjing	省级行政中心 Provincial-level administrative center	地区界 Regional boundary		大巴山 Dabashan Mt.	山脉名 Mountain
◎ 镇江 Zhenjiang	地级行政中心 Prefecture-level administrative center	军事分界线 Military demarcation line		台湾岛 Taiwan Is.	岛屿 Island
● 六合 Liuhe	县级行政中心 County-level administrative center	高速公路 Highway		塔里木盆地 Tarim Basin	盆地 Basin
○ 谢集 Xieji	一般居民地 Local-level administrative center	国道 National highway		腾格里沙漠 Tenggeli Desert	沙漠 Desert
◉ 平壤 P'yŏngyang	外国首都 Foreign capital	一般公路 Road			
◎ 新义州 Sinŭiju	外国大中城市 Foreign large and medium size city	铁路 Railroad		—125—	经纬线 Longitude, latitude
○ 沙里院 Sariwŏn	外国一般城市 Foreign city	通航河段 Canal		北回归线 Tropic of cancer	北回归线 Tropic of Cancer
	国界、未定国界 National boundary Undefined international boundary	✈ 双流国际机场 Shuangliu International Airport	机场 Airport	至马尼拉1565海里 To Manila 1565n miles	航海线 Shipping route
	省级界 Provincial boundary	⚓ 天津港 Tianjin pt.	港口 Port	▲ 长城 Great Wall	世界自然和文化遗产 UNESCO World Natural and Cultural Heritage Site
	河流、湖泊 River and lake	▲ 泰山 Taishan hill	山峰 Summit	✿ 九寨沟 Jiuzhaigou	国家重点风景名胜区 National scenic area

城市平面图
City Map Legend

4

江苏省地图 MAP OF JIANGSU PROVINCE

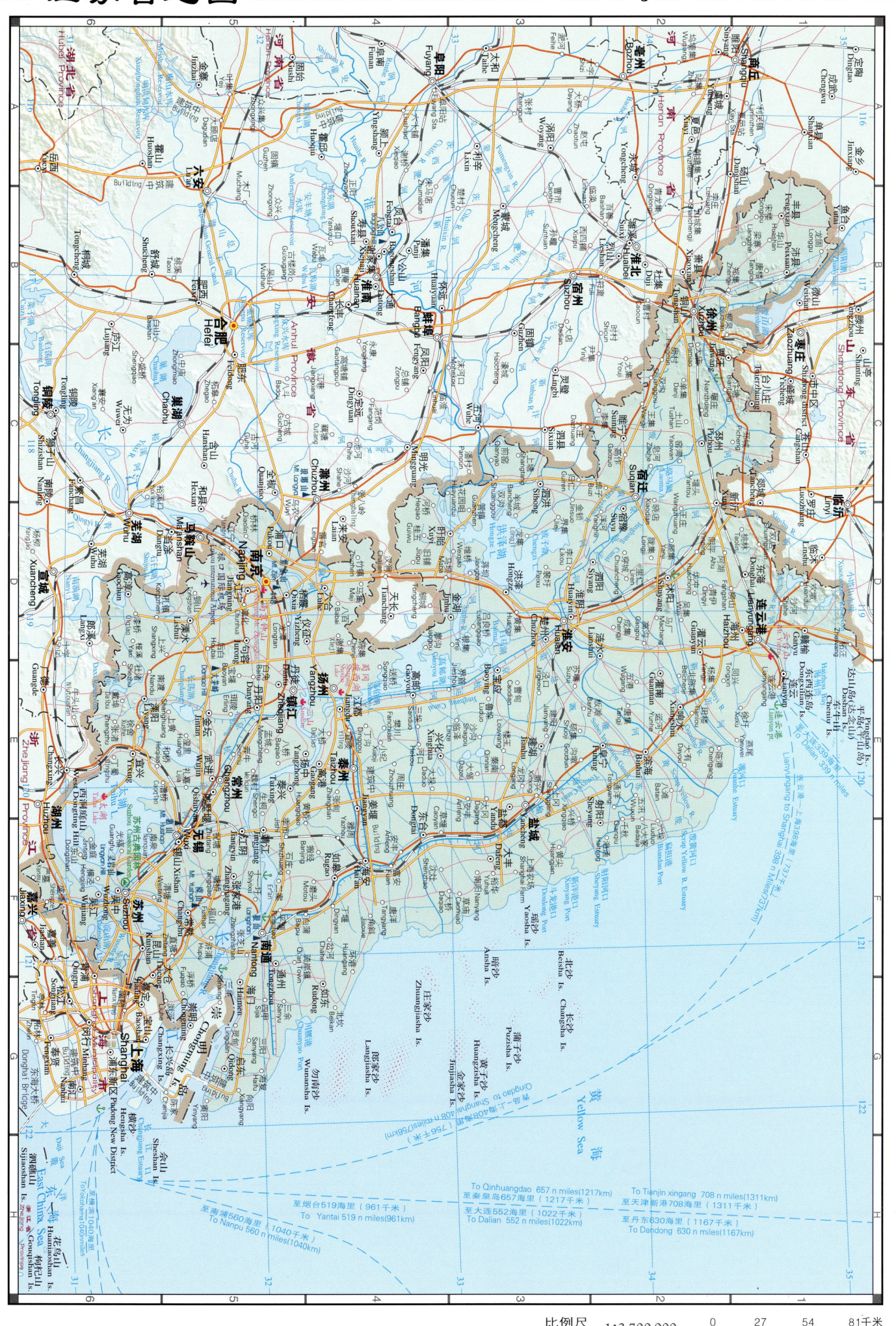

南京地图
MAP OF NANJING

The Temple of Confucius (Fuzi Miao) and the nearby canal attract many visitors to Nanjing.

Old people relaxing, southern Jiangsu

Jiangsu Province is located in the plains of the Yangtze River Delta, bordering Shandong Province to the north, Anhui Province to the west, Zhejiang Province to the south, and the city of Shanghai to the southeast. The provincial capital is Nanjing

Provincial Overview

The water towns in southern Jiangsu are known for their gardens, canals, and silk production, attracting millions of visitors each year.

Jiangsu In Brief

Origin

Jiāngsū 江苏 Province as it stands today was more or less established during the Qīng 清 Dynasty (1616 - 1911), under the name Jiāngnán 江南 in 1666. The province's current name combines "jiāng 江" from Jiāngníng 江宁 (present day Nánjīng 南京) and "sū 苏" from Sūzhōu 苏州. The city is referred to as "Sū" for short.

Administrative Division

The province is located in the plains of the Yangtze River Delta, bordering Shāndōng 山东 Province to the north, Ānhuī 安徽 Province to the west, Zhèjiāng 浙江 Province to the south, and Shànghǎi 上海 to the southeast. Jiāngsū contains 13 prefecture-level divisions, which are subsequently divided into 106 county-level divisions. The province covers an area of 102,000 sq km.

Population

As of the 2007 census, Jiāngsū's population was 72,530,000, making it the 5th most populated province in China.

The Capital

The provincial capital is Nánjīng 南京. Nánjīng is known as "the ancient capital of ten dynasties," and was the country's political center before 1949. Nánjīng is divided into 11 districts and two counties and has an area of 6,501 sq km, and a population of 5.97 million. Situated on the Yangtze River Delta, Nánjīng houses the largest inland port in China.

Terrain

The province is located across two geological units: the North China platform and the Yangtze Meta-platform. Plains cover more than half of this flat, low-lying province; most of Jiāngsū hovers around 50 m above sea level. Jiāngsū borders the Yellow Sea to the east and the Yangtze River cuts through the province in the south. Besides the Yangtze River, the longest river in China, Jiāngsū is also home to Lake Tài 太, Lake Hóngzé 洪泽, Lake Gāoyóu 高邮, Lake Luòmǎ 骆马, and Lake Yángchéng 阳澄.

Climate

Jiāngsū is located in a transit belt between the subtropics and the warm temperate zone. There are frequent rains between spring and summer, and typhoons and rainstorms in the late summer and early autumn. The annual average rainfall is 800 - 1200 mm,

With two fifths of the Grand Canal running through the province, Jiangsu has benefited greatly from trade and commerce. The prosperity in turn has made the local population one of China's most well-educated.

most of which occurs during the summer monsoon season.

History and Culture

During the earliest dynasties, the area known as Jiāngsū was home to an ancient ethnic group, the Huái Yí 淮夷, and was far removed from Chinese civilization. Even during China's golden age of the Hàn 汉 Dynasty (206 B.C.E - 220 C.E.), the province remained a backwater area. It wasn't until the development of the wealthy mercantile class and market economy during the Sòng 宋 Dynasty (960 - 1279 C.E.) that Jiāngsū finally hit its mark as a center of trade. The southern cities, especially Sūzhōu and Yángzhōu 扬州, would eventually become synonymous with luxury and opulence in China.

The area became so well known that in Chinese, ancient expressions emerged such as "Heaven above, Sūzhōu and Hángzhōu 杭州 below" and "The harvests of Sūzhōu and Húzhōu 湖州 can feed the nation." The area's superior silk quickly became a coveted item among China's wealthy and elite. The growth of commerce and industry continued into the Míng 明 (1368 - 1644) and Qīng (1616 - 1911) dynasties and led to southern Jiāngsū's emergence as one of China's major cultural centers. Moreover, Nánjīng was chosen as the capital of the Míng Dynasty, though the capital

Suzhou houses many well-preserved traditional Chinese gardens. Now a UNESCO Cultural Heritage Site; the gardens were built mainly in the Ming Dynasty when the city underwent considerable economic growth and flourished as a place of refinement.

Yuejiang Lou of Nanjing overlooking the Yangtze River. Nanjing is known as "the ancient capital of ten Chinese dynasties."

was soon moved to Běijīng 北京 following a coup.

Modern-day Jiāngsū and Ānhuī 安徽 were collectively called Nánzhílì 南直隶 during the Míng Dynasty, a territory governed directly by the central government. In the Qīng Dynasty, Nánzhílì was established as Jiāngnán Province, and Jiāngsū and Ānhuī were eventually separated.

During the early 20th century, after the formation of the Republic of China and while China was being torn apart by warlords, Jiāngsū changed hands several times. But in 1927, Nánjīng became the central base of power once more, this time for the government headed by Chiang Kai-shek (Jiǎng Jièshí 蒋介石). Nánjīng would eventually fall during the Sino-Japanese War and be subject to atrocities by the occupying Japanese forces. That three-month period is known as the Nánjīng Massacre. Nánjīng would be re-established as the capital of the Republic of China after the war's end in 1945. In 1949, when the Communists took power, the nation's capital was moved to Běijīng.

During the 1990s, the southern areas of Jiāngsū, particularly Sūzhōu and Wúxī 无锡, reaped the benefits of economic reforms spearheaded by Dèng Xiǎopíng 邓小平 (1904 - 1997). The income disparity between northern and southern Jiāngsū remains large.

Tourism

Visitors flock to the UNESCO-protected traditional Chinese gardens in Sūzhōu. Marco Polo described the canal city as the "Venice of the East." Yángzhōu's Shòuxī Hú 瘦西湖 or "Slender West Lake" is another popular attraction, as is Lake Tài, which is famous for producing "tortured rocks," coveted decorative pieces for Chinese gardens.

Suzhou Pingtan

Sūzhōu Píngtán 苏州评弹 combines the arts of storytelling and singing. It is performed in the Sūzhōu dialect, popular in Sūzhōu and some other parts of Jiāngsū 江苏 and Zhèjiāng 浙江 provinces, as well as the city of Shànghǎi 上海.

The art form began as early as the Táng 唐 Dynasty, a time when storytelling was well-received in teahouses across the country. In the Míng 明 and Qīng 清 dynasties, storytelling performances were performed in the Sūzhōu dialect, which is known for its delicacy. It was at this time that actors also began to sing during performances. Thus, all actors were required to play at least one traditional Chinese musical instrument, such as the pípa 琵琶, sānxián 三弦 (a three-stringed plucked instrument), and bǎn 板 (wooden clappers).

Today, many Jiāngsū locals still go to a teahouse nearly every day and spend a few hours enjoying the Sūzhōu Píngtán. They value this activity as one of life's best pleasures.

Pingtan actresses in a Qing Dynasty woodblock painting

Fast Facts

Formal Name: Jiāngsū Province

Short Name: Sū 苏

Symbols:
Flower: Jasmine or mòlìhuā 茉莉花
Tree: Gingko or yínxìng 银杏

Land Size: Jiāngsū has a land mass of 102,000 sq km, roughly the size of Cuba

Location: The plains of the Yangtze River Delta, eastern China

Border Provinces: Shāndōng 山东, Ānhuī 安徽, Zhèjiāng 浙江, and Shànghǎi 上海

Population: 72.53 million (2007)

Famous For: Traditional Chinese gardens, Sūzhōu, Lake Tài, Yángzhōu, Silk

Languages: Mandarin Chinese (Pǔtōng huà 普通话), Wú 吴 dialect

Photo taken of a rapeseed field in one of the suburbs of Nanjing, Jiangsu's provincial capital

Plants and Animals

Jiāngsū 江苏 does not have many wild animals, but the province does have plenty of aquatic resources. Its coastal fishing grounds are filled with yellow-fin tuna, hairtail, pomfret, shrimp, crabs, seashells and algae.

- 140 varieties of freshwater fish
- 600 types of wild plants

Fishermen taking part in a fishing competition on the Hongze Lake

Minerals

Jiāngsū is rich in a variety of mineral resources. One of the province's significant minerals is halite, which is essentially rock salt. The major energy resources include coal, petroleum and natural gas. The province's metallic resources include copper, lead, zinc, silver, gold, strontium and manganese. Non-metallic resources include sulphur, phosphorus, salt, quartz, cyanite, sapphire, diamond, kaolin, limestone, quartz sand, marble, and pottery clay.

- To date, 133 types of mineral resources have been discovered
- There are 8 kinds of mineral reserves

Water

Jiāngsū is home to some of the largest lakes in China, not to mention part of the country's mightiest source of water, the Yangtze River. Lake Tài 太 or Tàihú 太湖 alone, the largest lake in the province, holds over 4.6 billion cubic meters of water.

- Average annual precipitation is around 1,000 mm
- Lies along the upper reaches of five lakes
- Holds an abundant underground water source estimated at roughly 2.9 billion cubic meters/year (shallow layer) and 585 million cubic meters/year (coastal deep underwater)

Conservation

The province has paid closer attention to conservation recently, following a spate of criticism over pollution levels in popular attractions like Tàihú. Tàihú in particular is being treated for the algae bloom that now covers the lake's 2,435 sq km. Water from the Yangtze River was diverted to the scenic lake at a rate of 150 cubic meters/second in mid-2007 in efforts to dispel the bloom.

Père David's Deer

Location: Mostly in the nature reserves in the Yangtze River Delta, though they used to live in most parts of China.

Size: They can grow up to be 170 cm - 217 cm long, 122 cm - 137 cm high, and weigh up to 120 kg - 180 kg.

Food: Grass, weeds, and water plants

Home: Mostly in Dàfēng Mílù 大丰麋鹿 Nature Reserve

Habits: Social, good swimmers

Numbers: Over 1,000 in China (2006)

Status: Endangered species protected by Chinese and international law. They are now mostly found only in captivity.

Why is a Père David's Deer called sibuxiang in Chinese?

Père David's Deer (Latin: Elaphurus davidianus) is a strange-looking deer unique to China. It's called mílù 麋鹿 but more often referred to as sìbùxiàng 四不像, literally meaning "Four Unlikes." The animal has physical features resembling the hooves of an ox or niú 牛, the head of a horse or mǎ 马, the body of a donkey or lǘ 驴, and the antlers of a deer or lù 鹿.

Why is the Père David's Deer endangered?

Because of unrestricted hunting and a changing climate, the number of Père David's Deer has dropped drastically century after century. Deer in the wild went extinct during the Qīng 清 Dynasty (1616 - 1911). Before their extinction, Armand David, a French missionary, returned home from China with a number of the Père David's Deer. In the late 1980s, some deer were brought back from Britain to Jiāngsū's Dàfēng Mílù National Nature Reserve and have successfully multiplied there to over 1,000.

AGRICULTURE

A significant portion of Jiāngsū's economy comes from agriculture. Over recent years, the rural economy has developed at a clipped pace, with steady to rapid growth in crop production, livestock, and fisheries.

- Ranks second (after Húnán 湖南 Province) among rice producing provinces of China for rice yield
- Ranks first for oilseeds yield and second for cotton lint
- Has 260 types of fruit trees, tea plants, mulberry trees, and flowers

The many rivers and lakes have made Jiangsu historically known for its crabs, especially the ones called Dazha from the Yangcheng Lake.

To raise the production of rice and river shrimps respectively, farmers let them grow beside each other on one piece of land.

Provincial History

Jiangsu Rewind

L: Liú Bāng 刘邦, the first emperor of the Hàn 汉 Dynasty, a native of Jiāngsū 江苏 Province

E: Emma, a high school student from Chicago, Illinois, USA

By the time Emma checked into her hotel in Nánjīng 南京, Jiāngsū, it was already midnight. But Emma was too excited to sleep. Having studied the Chinese language and culture for two years, she knew that she had come to a place rich in history. Flipping through a book about Jiāngsū prepared by the hotel, she wasn't sure if she was awake or asleep. She saw a tall man coming to her in a long light-colored robe. From the way he dressed and his hairstyle, Emma could tell that he was from the Hàn Dynasty (206 B.C.E. - 220 C.E.).

L: Don't be afraid, Miss. I know you're a first time visitor to Jiāngsū, so I've come to chat with you.

E: No, I'm not afraid at all. Now I know who you are. You're Liú Bāng, the founder of the Hàn Dynasty. You lived even before Jesus Christ.

L: That's absolutely correct. My life was closely connected to the place that people today refer to as Jiāngsū Province.

E: Can you tell me something about the province's early history?

L: Don't rush. Let me first tell you something about how Jiāngsū got its name so that you can understand why this place has been so treasured throughout the generations. Geographically, most of Jiāngsū's land sits on plains with criss-crossing rivers. Jiāngsū ranks first out of all the Chinese provinces in terms of the number of rivers and lakes (2,900 rivers and over 300 lakes). Thus, the province best exemplifies a Chinese saying that describes the richness of a place — the land of fish and rice. Jiāngsū's abbreviation "Sū 苏" suggests that the formation of the character is fish plus rice. Jiāngsū was, and will always be, an agricultural cash cow for the Chinese nation.

E: Wow, Jiāngsū is fish and rice! That's interesting to know.

L: Actually, its early history was centered around Lake Tài 太 or Tàihú 太湖, an area especially suited for rice crops and aquiculture. As early as the Zhōu 周 Dynasty (1046 - 256 B.C.E.), two of King Tài's 太 three sons moved from northern China to the lake region, and they set up the State of Wú 吴 in today's Wúxī 无锡. Near the end of the Spring and Autumn Period, Wú became a great power and conquered other states. It was during this time that the Wú people started constructing a canal that connected Tàihú and other small rivers in the region. Because of this canal, the regional economy flourished immensely. Later, Emperor Yáng Dì 炀帝 of the Suí 隋 Dynasty (581 - 618 C.E.) was clearly aware of the canal's importance and extended it both southward and northward, constructing the marvel that is today called the Grand Canal.

E: What happened to Jiāngsū after Qín Shī Huáng 秦始皇 united China?

L: Jiāngsū became the battlefield for military warlords. I first aligned with Xiàng Yǔ 项羽, and together we ended the Qín 秦 Dynasty (221 - 206 B.C.E.). Later, I battled against Xiàng Yǔ. Eventually, I got the upper hand and ascended to the emperor's throne, starting the Hàn Dynasty.

E: I know Xiàng Yǔ from Director Chén Kǎigē's 陈凯歌 movie "Farewell My Concubine." What a tragic character!

L: Yes, but that's how history is meant to be, isn't it? Jiāngsū saw great development during the Hàn Dynasty. It was a relatively peaceful time and a golden age in Chinese history. But many wars broke out in the following Three Kingdoms Period as well as during the Western Jìn 晋 Dynasty (265 - 317 C.E.). The first major migration of Hàn Chinese took place in the Jìn Dynasty when aristocratic and well-educated Hàn families traveled from the north and settled down in Jiāngsū, Zhèjiāng 浙江, Ānhuī 安徽, and even Fūjiàn 福建 provinces. They brought with them not only advanced farming techniques but also a Confucian-based culture that emphasized the role of education.

Emperor Yang Di (center) of the Sui Dynasty has remained one of the most controversial historical figures.

The struggle between the Nationalist Party and the Communist Party finally came to an end when the former gave up Nanjing and retreated to Taiwan. In the photo, Chiang Kai-shek (left) met with Mao Zedong (right) during the Chongqing Negotiation held between the two parties in 1945.

Much of China's modern history was centered at the Presidential Palace (Zongtong Fu), Nanjing. In 1912, Sun Yat-sen was inaugurated as President of China here and his successor Chiang Kai-shek also had his offices in the compound.

Considered the Father of Modern China, Sun Yat-sen (1866 - 1925) is loved for his firm beliefs in what he called the Three Principles of the People: minzu (nationalism), minquan (democracy), and minsheng (people's livelihood).

E: I learned about this period of history while I was visiting Ānhuī. It was interesting for me to see what a crucial role Confucianism played in the emergence of the Huī 徽 (Southern Ānhuī) Culture.

L: You're so bright and correct! The spread of Confucianism has helped the people in Jiāngsū to become better educated, and this in turn sped up Jiāngsū's economic and cultural growth. The Suí and Táng 唐 dynasties saw another golden age in Jiāngsū. In particular, with the completion of the Grand Canal, northern Jiāngsū became a buffer of sorts between northern and southern China, whereas southern Jiāngsū emerged as a trade and cultural center. The prosperity lasted into the Sòng 宋 Dynasty (960 - 1279 C.E.), when cities like Yángzhōu 扬州 and Sūzhōu 苏州 were both synonymous with opulence.

E: What about Nánjīng? I've heard that it was the capital for many dynasties.

L: Nánjīng was formerly called Jiànkāng 建康 and was the capital for at least ten dynasties. It received its present-day name, meaning southern capital (as opposed to Běijīng 北京, meaning northern capital), when the Míng 明 Emperor Zhū Dì 朱棣 moved the empire's capital northward in an attempt to ward off invaders.

Jiāngsū was formally established in the 17th century. It remained a center of national importance for Míng and Qīng 清 rulers. It was estimated that one sixth of the country's revenue came from Jiāngsū. The flourishing textile industry helped Shànghǎi 上海, a former fishing village in Jiāngsū, to grow into a metropolis of trade and banking, and eventually into an independent municipality.

E: What was Jiāngsū's role after the fall of the Qīng Empire in 1911?

L: Good question. After the downfall of the Qīng Empire, there were no more emperors. The Republic of China, founded by the Nationalist Party, was established to take its place. In 1927, the party's founding father, Sūn Zhōngshān 孙中山 (Sun Yat-sen, 1866 - 1925) was succeeded by Jiǎng Jièshí 蒋介石 (Chiang Kai-shek, 1887 - 1975), who moved the government from Běijīng back to Nánjīng. Nánjīng remained China's capital until 1937, when Japan invaded China. Jiǎng Jièshí's government was then relocated to Chóngqìng 重庆, now another Chinese municipality. Nánjīng was in the hands of Wāng Jīngwèi 汪精卫, who collaborated with Japan. Records show that in 1937, when Nánjīng fell to the Japanese, 300,000 Nánjīng civilians died in the atrocity known as the Nánjīng Massacre.

After the war ended in 1945, Nánjīng was once again China's capital, and China entered into a period of struggles between the Nationalist and Communist parties. The last and decisive battle was fought in northern Jiāngsū in 1949. The Communist army's crossing

The Nanjing Massacre was one of the worst genocide crimes in history. It was reported that in Nanjing alone, over 300,000 Chinese civilians were killed by the Japanese army during World War II.

of the Yangtze River and takeover of Nánjīng marked the end of the Nationalist rule over mainland China. Jiǎng Jièshí retreated to Táiwān 台湾 to continue heading the Republic of China. When the People's Republic of China was founded in 1949, the Communist Party chose Běijīng for its capital, and Nánjīng was made into the provincial capital of Jiāngsū.

E: What a history! What about today's Jiāngsū?

L: Jiāngsū benefited much from the economic reforms initiated by the former Chinese leader Dèng Xiǎopíng 邓小平 (1904 - 1997). Southern Jiāngsū is part of the Yangtze River Development Delta, with Sūzhōu and Wúxī taking the lead. The two cities are among the top ten cities in terms of gross domestic product (GDP). But the speedy growth, especially that achieved by the township and private businesses, comes at the expense of water and air pollution. This is a serious issue for Jiāngsū.

E: I hope that people's environmental awareness enables Jiāngsū to forever remain the "land of fish and rice."

When Emma suddenly woke up, she found herself sleeping with all her clothes on, her face covered by the book she had been reading that night. "How I wish I could actually meet the guy in my dream, a Chinese emperor!" Emma thought to herself.

Explore-A-Province in China®

Famous Political Figures from Jiangsu

Liú Bāng 刘邦 (256 - 195 B.C.E.)

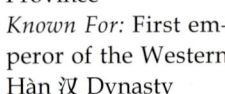

AKA: Hàn Gāozǔ 汉高祖, Pèi Gōng 沛公
From: Pèi 沛 County (today's Fēng 丰 County), Jiāngsū 江苏 Province
Known For: First emperor of the Western Hàn 汉 Dynasty

Liú Bāng was the first person from an ordinary family background to become a Chinese emperor. He was born to farmers and served as a low-level official during the late years of the Qín 秦 Dynasty (221 - 206 B.C.E.), a period of history marked by numerous uprisings. Liú Bāng joined one uprising troop and soon rose to become its leader under the title of Pèi Gōng, meaning Master from Pèi County. In 206 B.C.E, Liú Bāng and his army ended the Qín's reign by first setting foot upon Xián Yáng 咸阳, the Qín's capital. In the following years, he and Xiàng Yǔ 项羽, another rebellious leader from today's Jiāngsū, fought to gain complete control of all the land. Xiàng Yǔ outnumbered Liú Bāng in troops and got the upper hand in their fight for supremacy. However, with determination, wit, and teamwork, Liú Bāng finally managed to defeat Xiàng Yǔ at Gāixià 垓下. In 202 B.C.E., he made himself the first emperor of the Hàn Dynasty (206 B.C.E. - 220 C.E.) in Xián Yáng, which he renamed Cháng'ān 长安 (today's Xī'ān 西安 in Shaanxi Province). He believed that Confucianism was more effective in governance than laws. He also took effective measures to cut taxes and hired more people from ordinary family backgrounds to become state officials. This made Liú Bāng quite popular among Chinese historians.

Xiàng Yǔ 项羽 (232 - 202 B.C.E.)

AKA: Xī Chǔ Bà Wáng 西楚霸王 (Prince of Western Chǔ 楚)
From: Sùqiān 宿迁, Jiāngsū Province
Known For: Liú Bāng's rival, a general with outstanding physical strength

Peking Opera mask for Xiang Yu

Xiàng Yǔ came from a noble family that lived in the State of Chǔ. Because of the early deaths of both parents, he was raised by his uncle Xiàng Liáng 项梁, who encouraged the boy to study martial arts. Later, both the uncle and cousin joined one of the uprising forces and soon took over the troops' leadership. After his uncle's death, Xiàng Yǔ and his army aligned with other forces, including Liú Bāng's, with the intention of toppling the Qín Dynasty. Though one minute later than Liú Bāng to enter the Qín capital of Xián Yáng, Xiàng Yǔ was still able to rule the country. He divided the empire into 18 principalities and made himself king of the largest one. This caused a five-year struggle known as the Chǔ Hàn 楚汉 Contention between him and Liú Bāng. Xiàng Yǔ met his end when he lost the battle at Gāixià 垓下. From this event came the famous story "Farewell My Concubine." Because of Xiàng Yǔ's bravery and immense physical strength, he has been revered as a popular cultural hero throughout the ages. On the other hand, because of his blunt nature, he is also known as a ruler who lacked leadership in the areas of management, political diplomacy, and human resource issues.

Lǐ Yù 李煜 (937 - 978 C.E.)

AKA: Lǐ Hòuzhǔ 李后主, Lǐ Chóngguāng 李重光, Liánfēng Jūshì 莲峰居士
From: Xúzhōu 徐州, Jiāngsū
Known For: Last ruler of the Southern Táng 唐 Kingdom, Cí 词 poet

Lǐ Yù was the last ruler of the Southern  Táng Kingdom between 961 and 975 C.E., a time when China was torn apart into many kingdoms (in the Five Dynasties and Ten Kingdoms Period). He and his family were kept captive for many years by the Sòng 宋 Emperor Tàizōng 太宗 before he was poisoned in 978 C.E.

Though a mediocre king and a tragic figure, he is remembered today as a master of Cí poetry. Some of his greatest poems were written while in captivity. In his poems, he laments the loss of his kingdom and the old days of his former pleasure-seeking life. His Cí poetry broadens the genre by also writing about history and philosophy.

Zhōu Ēnlái 周恩来 (1898 - 1976)

AKA: Zhōu Xiángyǔ 周翔宇
From: Huái'ān 淮安, Jiāngsū
Known for: The people's premier to the Chinese, a gifted and accomplished diplomat outside China

Born to a well-educated couple in Shàoxīng 绍兴, Zhèjiāng 浙江 Province, Zhōu Ēnlái was given to his uncle to be his stepson at an early age and thus spent most of his early years in Huái'ān, Jiāngsū Province. During his school years in Tiānjīn 天津, his time was mostly given to students' movements aiming at crushing and defeating warlords and imperialism. He was an activist during the May Fourth Movement. His political vision broadened when he stayed in Europe in the early 1920s. He returned to China to work as Director of the Communist Guǎngdōng 广东 Military Affairs Department. He quickly worked himself up to be elected to the CCP Politburo at the age of 29. His marriage to Dèng Yǐngchāo 邓颖超, a revolutionary from Tiānjīn, took place in 1925. As they had no children of their own, the couple eventually raised several orphaned children of "revolutionary martyrs." Among them former Premier Lǐ Péng 李鹏 was the most famous.

Between the 1930s and 1940s, Zhōu acted as the CCP spokesperson and was responsible for dealing with the rival Nationalist Party members. It was also during this time that Zhōu Ēnlái firmly sided with Máo Zédōng 毛泽东 (1893 - 1976) and helped him rise to the highest chair in the Communist Party.

Zhōu Ēnlái served as the country's premier for the new Communist China starting in 1949 until his death in 1976. He also served as the country's Minister of Foreign Affairs for quite some time. He called for "peaceful co-existence" at the Geneva Conference (1953) and the Bandung Conference (1955), and he was a moderate force during the Cold War years. Known as a trusted diplomat, Zhōu Ēnlái was one of the most important key players responsible for resuming ties with the Western world. In 1972, he greeted US President Richard Nixon, and the two jointly signed the *Shànghǎi 上海 Communiqué*.

As Premier, Zhōu Ēnlái made great efforts in developing the country's economy, but any signs of progress were quickly thwarted by ongoing political movements carried out by Máo Zédōng (Chairman Máo). Though Zhōu Ēnlái worked hard to make changes to Máo's leftist campaigns including the disastrous Great Leap Forward (1958 - 1960) and the Cultural Revolution (1966 - 1976), the country did undergo serious economic setbacks. It was only in his last years (in 1975) that Zhōu Ēnlái was able to push for the "Four Modernizations." Just prior to his death in 1976, he made his last effort in getting Dèng Xiǎopíng 邓小平 (1904 - 1997) appointed as First Deputy Premier.

Jiāng Zémín 江泽民 (b. 1926)

From: Yángzhōu 扬州, Jiāngsū Province
Known For: Former President (1993 - 2003) of the People's Republic of China

Jiāng Zémín came from a distinguished family that formerly resided in the area historically known as Huīzhōu 徽州 in southern Ānhuī 安徽 Province. Eight Táng 唐 Dynasty (618 - 907 C.E.) ministers came from the Jiāng 江 clan.

Jiāng Zémín entered politics, from an engineering background, as Minister of the Electronics Industry. In 1985, he became mayor of Shànghǎi and eventually the Party Chief of Shànghǎi. Though he received mixed reviews of his work as mayor, he eventually made the move to national politics and rose to power in the wake of the student protests known as the 1989 Tiān'ānmén 天安门 Movement. He became president in 1993 and spent most of his time as leader introducing and supporting substantial reforms. While he was in office, Hong Kong and Macau were returned to China.

Hú Jǐntāo 胡锦涛 (b. 1942)

From: Jiāngyàn 姜堰, Jiāngsū Province
Known For: Currently President (2003 -) of the People's Republic of China

Hú Jǐntāo's family migrated from southern Ānhuī to Jiāngsū during his grandfather's generation. In 1965, he received his BS degree in hydraulic engineering at Tsinghua University and became a Communist party member. He worked through the party ranks to eventually lead the Communist Youth League in the early 1980s. Then, he worked in China's poorer regions including Gānsū 甘肃 and Tibet. In the 1990s, he was chosen by China's top leaders as an ideal candidate to ensure the smooth transition of power. Actually, he became the youngest member of the CPC's Politburo Standing Committee, responsible for the Party's ideological work. The peaceful transition took place in 2002 when Hú Jǐntāo was elected Party General Secretary. With Wēn Jiābǎo 温家宝 (b. 1942), China's Premier since 2003, Hú Jǐntāo proposed "a Harmonious Society" aiming at equality among classes and fewer environmental damage caused by rapid economic growth. He also called for the modernization of the Communist Party, allowing both the middle bourgeoisie and the wealthy to become party members.

Jiangsu Timeline

Paleolithic Period (2.5 mil. - 10000 B.C.E.)
- The "Tāngshān 汤山 Ape-man" lives in Nánjīng 南京

Neolithic Period (8000 - 2100 B.C.E.)
- Qīngliángǎng 青莲岗 Culture in Huái'ān 淮安
- Cǎoxiéshān 草鞋山 Culture in Sūzhōu 苏州

Xià 夏 Dynasty (2070 - 1600 B.C.E.)

Shāng 商 Dynasty (1600 - 1046 B.C.E.)
- State of Wú 吴 is founded by Tài Bó 太伯 and Zhòng Yōng 仲雍

Zhōu 周 Dynasty (1046 - 256 B.C.E.)

Spring and Autumn Period (770 - 476 B.C.E.)
- The State of Wú becomes a powerful state under the leadership of Fūchài 夫差

Warring States Period (475 - 221 B.C.E.)
- The State of Qín defeats the State of Wú

Qín 秦 Dynasty (221 - 206 B.C.E.)
- Qín unifies China
- Uprisings led by Liú Bāng 刘邦 and Xiàng Yǔ 项羽

Hàn 汉 Dynasty (206 B.C.E. - 220 C.E.)
- Four Years' Contention between Liú Bāng and Xiàng Yǔ

Three Kindoms Period (220 - 280 C.E.)
- N nj ng becomes the capital of the W Kingdom

Western Jìn or Xī Jìn 西晋 (265 - 317 C.E.)
- Clans begin to move to southern China

Eastern Jìn or Dōng Jīng 东晋 (317 - 420)

Southern and Northern Dynasties (420 - 589 C.E.)

Suí 隋 Dynasty (581 - 618 C.E.)
- Emperor Yáng Dì 炀帝 extends the canal that the Wú people built to a marvel known as the Grand Canal
- Yángzhōu 扬州 becomes the economic center of China

Táng 唐 Dynasty (618 - 907 C.E.)
- A period of peace and stability - arts and literature flourish
- Ānshǐ 安史 Rebellion

Five Dynasties (907 - 960 C.E.)

Sòng 宋 Dynasty (960 - 1279 C.E.)
- Foreign tribes invade northern China
- The north and south border changes frequently
- Sūzhōu 苏州 replaces Yángzhōu as the national economic center

Yuán 元 Dynasty (1206 - 1368)
- Cotton and silk weaving workshops thrive in Jiāngsū 江苏

Míng 明 Dynasty (1368 - 1644)
- Emperor Zhūdì 朱棣 moves the capital from Nánjīng to Běijīng 北京
- Zhèng Hé 郑和 makes seven expeditions
- Zhèng Chénggōng 郑成功 expels the Dutch from Táiwān 台湾

Qīng 清 Dynasty (1616 - 1911)
- Tàipíng soldiers occupy and relocate Nánjīng the capital of their Heaven's State

The Republic of China (1912 - 1949)
- The Nationalist government makes Nánjīng once again its capital
- The Nánjīng Massacre takes place. 300,000 civilians are killed by Japanese Invaders
- Nánjīng is taken by Communist PLA on April 23rd, 1949

The People's Republic of China (1949 - present)
- The Great Leap Forward
- The Cultural Revolution
- Jiāngsū benefits from the reforms initiated by late Chinese leader Dèng Xiǎopíng
- Huáxī 华西 becomes the wealthiest village in China and a national model

Provincial Socioeconomy

Economics Chat

Jiangsu is home to some of the largest freshwater lakes in China, including the Taihu (pictured) and Hongze lakes.

E: Emma, high school student from Chicago touring Jiāngsū 江苏

W: Wú Gāng 吴刚 or Xiǎo Wú 小吴, tour guide and Jiāngsū native

Emma was sitting with her tour guide, Wú Gāng, in a taxi. It was her first night in Jiāngsū and she was curious about this new province.

E: Before I start sightseeing, can I ask you about Jiāngsū?

W: Of course!

THE LAND OF FISH AND RICE

E: I've heard that it is one of China's richest provinces. How come?

W: Location, location, location. Jiāngsū has two major rivers coursing through the province. The water not only makes for fertile plains, but the rivers themselves are also filled with resources. That's why the province is known as the "land of fish and rice," a place where there has always been plenty of work and food for its people.

Today, there's extensive irrigation in place to support cash crops like cotton, soybeans, sesame, and tea. Silkworms are also a big part of Jiāngsū's agriculture, and the area around Tàihú 太湖 (Lake Tài 太) is a major silk manufacturing base for China.

Beyond the food and textile industries, Jiāngsū is also known for its heavy industry, though this is pretty recent.

E: Why the switch?

W: Mostly because of Dèng Xiǎopíng's 邓小平 economic reforms. The development of heavy industry began after 1949, but it was Dèng's reforms that really pushed industrialism in the province during the 1990s. The impor-

Container depot at Liangyungang. The city is one of the world's top 100 container terminals.

Checking the quality of silk at the Suzhou Silk Factory. Southern Jiangsu, where Suzhou is located, is historically known as one of China's main silk production bases.

tant industries today are machinery, automobile, chemical, and electronic.

E: Has the entire province benefited from the economic reforms?

W: The benefits have been unequal. Southern cities close to Shànghǎi 上海, like Sūzhōu 苏州 and Wúxī 无锡, have become quite prosperous. They're among the top ten cities in China in terms of GDP, outstripping the provincial capital, Nánjīng 南京. There remains a large income disparity between northern and southern Jiāngsū.

The Richest Village in China

E: What else makes Jiāngsū stand out from the rest of the provinces?

W: Well, it's home to the "number one village in China," Huáxī 华西.

E: Number one for what?

W: Wealth! Huáxī was the first commune in China to list shares on the stock exchange in 1995.

E: Really? I thought only big private companies listed shares on stock exchanges.

W: Huáxī has certainly profited like a big private company. The village's fortune can be traced back to 1969, when a Communist Secretary founded a village-owned textile factory. This was a bold move during a time when China was pushing for more agricultural reforms. But the town slowly switched from agriculture to manufacturing. The move paid off, and the village has reported tens of billions of rénmínbì 人民币 (RMB) in turnover.

E: And what do residents get out of it?

W: Each Huáxī resident is like a shareholder in a company. Locals, all officially still registered as peasants, earn big bonuses and dividends every year on top of their annual salary. Their per capita income is seven times the national average.

Continued on page 18

Water towns, Chinese landscaped gardens, zigzag canals, arched bridges, and exquisite embroidery have all made Jiangsu a hot destination. Tourism contributes greatly to this picturesque province.

Young village ladies are hired to work in a small scale glove-making factory in Xiaoji Town, Yangzhou. Jiangsu is full of these factories set up either by collective communes or private owners.

Explore-A-Province in China

Behind the speedy economic growth, pollution is a serious problem that Jiangsu must deal with.

E: So everyone here is rich?

W: Yes and no. The wealth belongs to the commune, not to individuals: 80% of residents' bonuses and 95% of their dividends must be reinvested in the commune.

E: Do people resent having to give so much back?

W: It doesn't seem like it. The average living space is 450 square metres and each family has at least one car. They have health insurance and pensions. And now the village has become a model for socialism, so visitors and government officials are constantly pointing to Huáxī as the ideal. This must give locals a real sense of pride and accomplishment.

Provincial Tourism

E: Is tourism big in Jiāngsū?

W: Tourism contributes greatly to the provincial economy. People come here to experience the wonderful Wú 吴 culture. The cities of Nánjīng, Sūzhōu, Yángzhōu 扬州, and Wúxī, the Tàihú, the world famous traditional Chinese gardens, the foods, and folk arts are all big draws.

E: I can't wait for tomorrow to come.

Huaxi: the Wealthiest Village in China

What do Chinese farmers want in life? This question is best answered in a statement made by Wú Rénbǎo 吴仁宝, the former Village Chief who is now considered a national hero. "People here have five aims in life: money, a car, a house, a son, and respect. We give them that. Every family here is rich."

Wú Rénbǎo and his fellow villagers worked hard to make that dream come true. After 30 years of painstaking efforts, their village, called Huáxī 华西, situated in Jiāngyīn 江阴, Wúxī 无锡, has become the wealthiest village in China. In the 1980s, when most Chinese (especially farmers) were not market-oriented, Huáxī quickly moved its focus from agriculture to industry by setting up textile and steel factories. In the 1990s, Huáxī grabbed the chance to be the first Chinese community to list shares on a stock exchange.

Now the village owns 80 factories that employs 30,000 migrant workers to do most of the work for around 1,000 RMB a month. With the accumulated wealth, the village has been able to provide each local household a fully furnished villa of 400 sq m, a car, savings no less than one million RMB, free education for the village children, and free medical care — benefits that normal

Chinese farmers would love to have. This benevolence, however, has a price: all of a family's belongings and privileges would be taken away if the family decided to move out of the village.

Behind the utopian happiness, there are things visitors may find strange about Huáxī. Its villagers all live in houses that look the same. People are asked to go to the village administrative office to justify their expenditures. They have no weekends, no vacations and no privacy. There is no "nightlife" unless you sing Communist songs. There are no bars or coffee shops, no Internet cafés, and no karaokes.

Thus the hottest debate remains: can Huáxī's model be duplicated in other parts of China? Is it healthy for Chinese farmers to sacrifice their individuality and their independence in exchange for material wealth?

China's Political System and Government

Through the ages, China has always been unique in size, cultural diversity, world view and even its government. The vision of Máo Zédōng's 毛泽东 post-1949 "New China" spun the country into directions and alliances that were probably inconceivable to him as he set out on his vision to remake the nation as a "people's" government.

China's sheer size (9.6 million sq km) and home to over one fifth (1.3 billion people) of humanity demand a governance structure radically differing from Western models. The structure of the government is not neatly divided into executive and administrative branches. Instead, there are several divisions and organizations which interact and oversee one another, but which are fundamentally driven from the top down. The "top down" with the near absence of a lateral interaction is more than a character of government; it is a reflection of the Chinese culture, its traditions, and development through the ages.

Head of State

The president, as head of state, signs laws into order, appoints the premier, vice premiers, state councilors, ministers of various ministries and state commissions, the auditor-general, and the secretary-general of the State Council. These appointments accord with the decisions of the National Peoples Congress (NPC) and its Standing Committee. As well as conferring honorary titles of State and issuing orders of special amnesty, the president has the power to declare martial law, declare a state of war, and announce orders of general mobilization of the people's military.

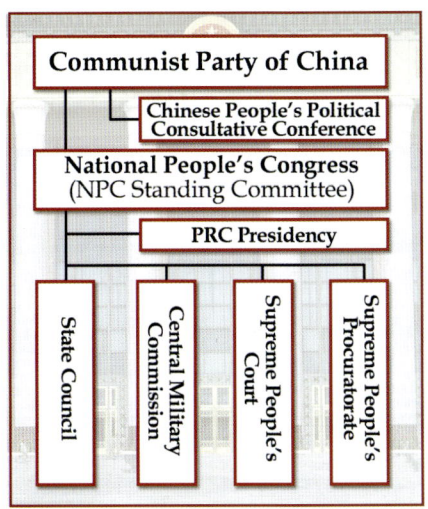

National People's Congress

The NPC is the governing organ of supreme power in the People's Republic of China. Its permanent body or group of leaders in office is called the Standing Committee. Both the NPC and its Standing Committee are elected for a term of five years through a process called "democratic centralism." A Chinese citizen exercises his/her right to vote at the local or county level, where elections determine the representatives or deputies to the NPC. Beyond the county level however, leadership positions are appointed (appointments are handed down by the next level of government, i.e. province to city, city to prefecture, prefecture to county). These appointments are ultimately subject to the NPC's approval. The NPC and its Standing Committee exercise the power of legislation, and in matters of election they retain the power to decide, supervise, appoint, and dismiss.

The State Council

The State Council, also known as the Central People's Government, is China's highest administrative body. It carries out the laws and decisions made by the NPC and is responsible for the running of the nation's day-to-day business. The State Council is made up of the Premier, Vice-Premiers, State Councilors and Ministers. Once again, these appointments are subject to the NPC's approval.

The Communist Party of China (CPC) was founded in 1921 in Shànghǎi 上海. It has been the party in power since 1949 when, under the leadership of Chairman Máo Zédōng, the People's Republic of China declared its nationhood in Tiān'ānmén 天安门 Square on October 1st of the same year.

Although the CPC has both central and local organizations, the Central Committee stands at the top of the organizational structure. Its General Secretary and the President of China have been the same person since 1983. The CPC nominates its Party's General Secretary for the position of Head of State (President), the nomination goes to the NPC for approval. In addition to his role as General Secretary, the President acts as Chairman of the Armed Forces and is assisted by vice-chairmen and a membership body under the title of **The Central Military Commission** of the PRC. The commission is elected for a term of five years after which its members can stand for re-election.

The Politburo (now 26 members) together with its Standing Committee undertakes the major decision-making of the CPC, as well as exercising the power of the Central Committee when that body is not in session. The CPC does not directly issue orders to organs of state power. What it does is put forward recommendations that are then exercised by the NPC.

A major advisory body to the CPC is **The Chinese People's Political Consultative Conference (CPPCC)**. It is a united front organization under the leadership of the Communist Party of China and includes the other eight non-communist parties. It also includes the **mass organizations** that represent groups within society such as the All-China Federation of Trade Unions, the Communist Youth League of China, and the All-China Women's Federation. These mass organizations basically function as liaisons between government, CPC, and the interest groups they represent, and work on a daily basis to benefit their constituencies. They meet annually in March or under special invitation from the CPC to draft white papers and submit suggestions to the Party and the State Council.

Local governments are responsible for running regional affairs and reporting to their superiors, i.e. county to prefecture to city to province to central government. Local democratic-style elections are held at the township and county levels enabling ordinary citizens to participate in governance.

Hong Kong and Macau are two special administrative regions which under "one country, two systems" function with more autonomy although in close consent with authorities in Běijīng 北京.

For the newcomer to all things Chinese, the barrage of government acronyms may seem confusing. The awkwardness can be accounted for however, when one visits this enormously diverse country where most people's lives are far from the government and politics of the capital. The day to day life of the average Chinese citizen is very much a product of Confucian ideals and operates from a distinctly Eastern sense of logic.

Provincial Capital

Nanjing, known as "the ancient capital for ten dynasties," is growing into a big modern city.

Experiencing Nanjing

Nánjīng 南京 is known as "the ancient capital of ten dynasties" (though some report that Nánjīng saw the rise and fall of only eight!). Today though, the city is more likely to see the rise of another skyscraper as it continues to emerge from the shadow of its big-city neighbor, Shànghǎi 上海. More and more people, local and foreign, are turning their attention to second-tier cities, and Nánjīng is one of these buzz locations.

Geography and Climate

Nánjīng is situated on the Yangtze River Delta. It is flanked by the Yangtze River in the west, and the Níngzhèn 宁镇 Ridge on the north, east, and south sides of the city. The former capital has a humid subtropical climate. It is one of the "Four Furnace-like Cities" in China; average summer temperatures hover around 35ºC, with the thermometer occasionally topping 40ºC. Monsoon season coincides with the summer heat, and the torrential rains drench everyone and everything in sight — though they do offer a respite from the scorching temperatures.

History

Nánjīng was the nation's capital in the early years of the Míng 明 Dynasty (1368 - 1644) and again in the early years of the Republic of China (1911 - 1937.) It was in Nánjīng that Sun Yat-sen (Sūn Zhōngshān 孙中山, 1866 - 1925), acting as provisional president, established a new republic that was henceforth to follow the Western solar calendar with its seven-day weeks instead of the traditional Chinese lunar one with its ten-day period. Sun Yat-sen has been called the "Father of the Revolution," the "Father of the Republic," and even the all-encompassing the "Father of Modern China." His lifelong desire was to overthrow the Qīng 清 Empire and modernize China following a Western mode. He finally succeeded when Emperor Pǔ Yí 溥仪 abdicated in 1912. Sun Yat-sen's historical footprint in Nánjīng is marked by an impressive memorial atop Purple Mountain.

Over two decades after Dr. Sun's revolutionary success, Nánjīng would lay witness to yet another historical event, though one much more somber. In 1937, the city was the site of one of history's most brutal massacres, which is frankly documented by historian Iris Chang (AKA Zhāng Chúnrú 张纯如) in her book *The Rape of Nanking*. The Nánjīng Massacre is commemorated at a haunting memorial in the southwestern part of town.

Transportation

Nánjīng is eastern China's transportation hub. The Lùkǒu 禄口 International Airport runs domestic flights and routes to nearby Japan, Korea, Thailand, and Singapore. The airport,

Nanjing offers good restaurants and a lively nightlife.

The statues at the Martyrs' Memorial were erected to commemorate those who lost their lives during the Chinese Revolution (1927 - 1949).

highways and railway station link Nánjīng to all the major cities in China, including Běijīng 北京 and Shànghǎi 上海. The Nánjīng South Railway Station started operation in 2008 and to date, will be the largest railway station in Asia upon completion.

As part of the Yangtze River Delta, Nánjīng also houses the largest inland port in China. The port's yearly output tops 65 million tons.

Highlights

Purple Mountain is dotted with no less than 85 tourist attractions and is a must-see for visitors to Nánjīng. The highlight is Dr. Sun Yat-sen's Mausoleum, a stark white building topped with blue tile roofs that you can admire from any one of the 392

Mochou Lake is a beautiful spot outside the city wall in western Nanjing.

steps leading to it. A trolley ride away is the XiàoLíng 孝陵 Tomb of Emperor Zhū Yuánzhāng 朱元璋 of the Míng Dynasty (1638 - 1644). On the other side of the mountain is Línggǔ 灵古 Temple. On a clear day, the top of Línggǔ Temple offers a bird's eye view of the surrounding mountain and the city.

For a festive atmosphere, there is the Confucian Temple downtown. Oversized statues of the stately philosopher and his loyal students are housed inside the temple, while an eclectic mix of modern shoppers and stores populate the lively streets outside the temple.

At the southwestern end of town, the Memorial Hall of the Victims in Nánjīng Massacre by Japanese Invaders is located on an execution and mass burial site from the Japanese invasion. The memorial's modern architecture is both abstract and brutally frank. It is a thought-provoking, moving visit.

Education and Research

Nánjīng has been an educational center for almost 2,000 years. It boasts some of the most prominent educational institutions in China, most notably Nánjīng University. The private Hopkins-Nánjīng University is a joint venture between Nánjīng University and John Hopkins University in Baltimore, Maryland. In total, Nánjīng has 48 colleges and universities and 508 scientific research institutions.

The Nánjīng Hi-Tech Zone is a government-ratified development area that concentrates on developing new

Stone sculptures along the Xiaoling Sacred Way to the Ming Tombs on the Purple Mountain (Zhongshan Mountain)

The Mausoleum of Dr. Sun Yat - sen (Sun Zhongshan) is a popular destination to pay homage to the man who is honored as the "Father of Modern China."

Known as "the ancient capital of ten dynasties," Nanjing has many cultural wonders from the past including the city walls. Part of the walls can still be walked along.

Fast Facts
Formal Name: Nánjīng 南京
AKA: Jīnlíng 金陵
Symbols: *Flower:* Plum blossom or méihuā 梅花 *Tree:* Deodar Cedar or xuěsōng 雪松
Land size: 6,501 sq km
Population: 5.97 million
Famous For: Being "an ancient capital of ten dynasties"

21

Explore-A-Province in China®

The Nanjing Yangtze River Bridge in the early 1970s. The bridge, completed in 1968, was a signature piece to represent one of the highest achievements of the Communist Party during the Cultural Revolution period.

and high-tech industries. It is home to over a thousand companies, such as the MG Factory (MG being the iconic British automobile), as well as the Nánjīng Software Park and Nánjīng Bio-Medicine Park.

MANUFACTURING AND INDUSTRY

Auto manufacturing is a dominant industry, with several companies having set up plants in Nánjīng. The Nánjīng Automobile (Group) Corporation is a state-owned enterprise and one of China's oldest automobile manufacturers. They own two Chinese brands (Soyat and Yuejin) as well as the formerly British MG. In 2007, Cháng'ān 长安, Mazda and Ford joined forces and opened China's most advanced automotive manufacturing plant at the time. Apart from cars, the electronics, petrochemical, iron, and steel industries are also very important to Nánjīng. The city is also the largest commercial center in China after Shànghǎi.

FUTURE DEVELOPMENT

Nánjīng's future is bright. As cities like Běijīng and Shànghǎi reach their saturation points, companies and investors are turning to second—tier cities like Nánjīng for development opportunities. The city's investment desirability gets a further boost from its four industrial parks. Nánjīng's GDP, however, still lags behind that of Wúxī 无锡 and Sūzhōu 苏州.

Iris Chang and the Nanjing Massacre

The Nánjīng 南京 Massacre was the atrocity committed by the Japanese invaders when they burned and looted China's then capital in 1937. It was estimated that over 300,000 Chinese citizens (mostly ordinary civilians and a small number of unarmed soldiers) were brutally killed. The details of the atrocity were revealed by Iris Chang (1968 - 2004), a Chinese American writer, when she published her most famous book *The Rape of Nanking*. A New York Times Bestseller for months, the book was the first English non-fiction to deal extensively on the mass killing during the Nánjīng Massacre. Sadly, writing *The Rape of Nanking* caused Iris Chang personal suffering. One day in November 2004, she was found dead in her car on a remote California road. While presumed to be a suicide, her death remains unclear to this day.

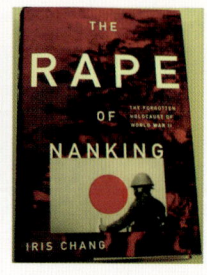

Jiangsu City Life

SUZHOU

Location: Southeastern Jiāngsū 江苏
Population: 6.06 million
Size: 6,267 sq km (2,419.1 sq mile)

Sūzhōu 苏州 is a popular tourist destination, having once been dubbed the "Venice of the East" by Marco Polo. While the canals hold a certain charm, the city's main attractions are the UNESCO-protected traditional Chinese gardens. The city's long standing as a textile hub means that tourists often pick up Sūzhōu silk, especially embroidery work. Historically, the Sūzhōu region was the birthplace of Kūnqǔ 昆曲 Opera, which has also come under UNESCO protection.

Suzhou

WUXI

Location: Southern end of Jiāngsū 江苏
Population: 4.53 million
Size: 4,785 sq km (1,847 sq mile)

Legend has it that Wúxī 无锡 was a mining town that exhausted its tin deposits, hence its name, which literally means "without tin." Wúxī's main attraction is Tàihú 太湖 or Lake Tài 太, which has unfortunately suffered from copious amounts of pollution in recent years.

Wuxi

Yangzhou

Location: Mid-western Jiāngsū, on the northern bank of Yangtze River
Population: 4.57 million
Size: 6,634 sq km (2,561 sq mile)

Yángzhōu 扬州 dates back to the Spring and Autumn Period (770 - 476 B.C.E.), and until as recently as the 19th century, it was a major trade exchange for salt, rice and silk. Yángzhōu as it now stands took form mostly during the Míng 明 Dynasty (1368 - 1644). The later Qīng 清 Dynasty (1616 - 1911) brought riots and war to the Jiāngsū 江苏 city, leading to Yángzhōu's decline and loss of status as China's leading economic center. Today, it is best known for the picturesque Slender West Lake and its surrounding traditional architecture.

Yangzhou

Xuzhou

Location: Northwestern Jiāngsū
Population: 9.17 million
Size: 11,260 sq km (4,346 sq miles)

Xúzhōu's 徐州 history can be traced back to 4000 C.E. Due to its strategic location connecting Jiāngsū, Shāndōng 山东, Hénán 河南 and Ānhuī 安徽 provinces, it has been significant for military strategists and Chinese leaders since ancient times. It is estimated that over 200 famous battles were fought there. Xúzhōu is the home city to Liú Bāng 刘邦, the first Hàn 汉 Dynasty Emperor, and his rival, Xiàng Yǔ 项羽, the King of the State of Chǔ 楚. The city of Xúzhōu is dotted with cultural and historical relics and remains, among them the bas-reliefs of the Hàn Dynasty, the Museum of Hàn Warriors and Horse Figurines, and the Gǔpéng 古彭 Square are must-sees for visitors. Destroyed several times throughout history, the ancient city of Xúzhōu is now multi-layered.

Xuzhou

Thus, Xúzhōu is also known as the "Pompeii of the Orient."

Lianyungang

Location: Northeastern Jiāngsū by the East China Sea, facing Japan and South Korea
Population: 4.72 million
Size: 7,444 sq km (2,873 sq miles)

A famous port city, Liányúngǎng 连云港 is rich in water resources that cover one fourth of the region's total area. The region has historically well-developed agriculture and fishery industries. Still a major portion of the city's income, agriculture nowadays has shifted to high-tech organic planting. Of the many beautiful natural sights in Liányúngǎng, Huāguǒshān 花果山 is the most popular destination. Huāguǒshān or Flowers and Fruits Mountain earned its recognition from one of the Chinese Four Classical Novels, *Journey to the West* or Xīyóujì 西游记. The author, Wú Chéng'ēn 吴承恩, made the mountain the home of Monkey King or Sūnwùkōng 孙悟空. Dōnghǎi 东海 in Liányúngǎng is known as China's Crystal Center, since it is the country's biggest producer of crystal.

Lianyungang

Changzhou

Location: Southern Jiāngsū on the Yangtze River, between Nánjīng 南京 and Shànghǎi 上海
Population: 3.5 million
Size: 4,180 sq km (1,613 sq miles)

Bordering Zhènjiāng 镇江 to the west and Wúxī to the east, Chángzhōu 常州 is almost equidistant (about 150 km) from both Nánjīng and Shànghǎi, and it lies south of the Yangtze River. The Great Canal, which passes through the city, has contributed greatly to making the city picturesque with its canals, rivers, and lakes. The old lanes along the canals have changed little, a testimony to the city's 2500-year glorious past. Among the many attractions, the Tiānníng 天宁 Temple, and the China Dinosaur Park completed in 2000 are big draws for visitors. In addition, Chángzhōu, which has been a historical center for the textile industry, still contributes greatly to Jiāngsū's GDP.

Changzhou

Yancheng

Location: Central and eastern Jiāngsū
Population: 8 million
Size: 14,562 sq km (5,621 sq miles)

Yánchéng's 盐城 history dates back 2100 years. The city's name literally means Salt City, and this simple yet precious natural commodity has always helped Yánchéng maintain its prominence since the Hàn 汉 Dynasty. Today, wetlands in Yánchéng represent one seventh of the country's total wetland area, and are home to numerous animals including the precious red-crowned crane, and Père David's Deer. Yánchéng is also known as the national center for the production of fireworks and firecrackers.

Yancheng

Provincial People

A traditional Chinese wedding held in southern Jiangsu

An Oral Portrait

One afternoon, Emma and her tour guide, Wú Gāng 吴刚 or Xiǎo Wú 小吴, visited the Museum of Opera and Theater, located in downtown Sūzhōu 苏州. It was housed in a beautiful Míng 明 Dynasty building made of latticed wood and contained a nice collection of old musical instruments and Kūnqǔ 昆曲 opera costumes. Emma couldn't move her eyes away from the embroidered silk costumes. All she could do was gasp in awe at every fine stitch on the pieces. After the visit, Xiǎo Wú invited Emma to a teahouse nearby the museum. Comfortably seated, Emma couldn't wait to ask Xiǎo Wú to tell her something about the people of Jiāngsū 江苏. Here was how Xiǎo Wú presented his provincial people:

It's no wonder that each visitor to Sūzhōu can't help admiring the exquisite gardens, elegant Kūnqǔ Opera, delicious Sū 苏 (Sūzhōu) cuisine, and highly accomplished Sū embroidery. Those who created all these marvels are from a refined area famous for its Wú 吴 culture. This culture originated south of the Yangtze River (Chángjiāng 长江), along Tàihú 太湖 (Lake Tài 太). Renowned as a "land of fish and rice," the region has been blessed with abundant resources and very few natural disasters. Its prosperity was crucial in helping southern Jiāngsū, where the Wú culture is dominant, develop into an influential cultural center. This explains why southern Jiāngsū has been home to some of China's greatest artists (Měi Lánfāng 梅兰芳, Zhèng Xiè 郑燮, and Táng Yín 唐寅), most renowned scholars, highest political leaders (Zhōu Ēn'lái 周恩来, Jiāng Zémín 江泽民, and Hú Jǐntāo 胡锦涛), and richest merchants.

In general, people in southern Jiāngsū have a mild temperament. This character trait is reflected when locals begin to talk. They speak the Wú dialect (Wúyǔ 吴语). With an approximate number of 100 million speakers, it is the second most commonly spoken dialect after Madarin. Wúyǔ is reputed to sound soft, light, and flowing. The dialect's softness has given local people the image of being "mild-mannered." Another example of their soft and light side is seen in the people's cuisine. The sweet and sour taste, a typical flavor, makes Sūzhōu cuisine stand out. When it comes to describing the local women, the aforementioned adjectives such as "mild" and "soft" bear more positive connotations than negative ones. Soft physical features, slim body shape, and nice temperament have all made the women the epitome of traditional southern beauty. Another interesting point worth mentioning is that both men and women in the region have a reputation for their business savvy and deft ability to work with their hands. The region boasts the most powerful business people and the best artisans. The combination of both qualities has actually helped Shànghǎi 上海 quickly emerge into the nation's economic and central hub since the majority of Shànghǎi's population emigrated from southern Jiāngsū.

Along the Yangtze River sits Nánjīng 南京 and Yangzhou 扬州. Geographically

Selling buns that are arranged in the shape of yin and yang in central Jiangsu

Old man making a bamboo basket at his house in southern Jiangsu. The traditionally well-built house tells something about the man's family background.

Girl doing homework. She lives with her family on a fishing boat. The family lives on catches from the Hongzehu (lake), northwestern Jiangsu.

An experienced Huaiyang cuisine chef in Yangzhou

speaking, this region in Jiāngsū is centrally located. Thus, the "neither-northern-nor-southern" location gives its people a chance to infuse both cultures.

The region north of the Yangtze River is historically influenced by the Chǔ 楚 culture. Chǔ was a powerful state during the Warring States Period, Qín 秦, and Hàn 汉 dynasties, and the Three Kingdoms Period. The region was strategically sought-after by military strongmen in various periods of history. Numerous famous generals, including Liú Bāng 刘邦, Xiàng Yǔ 项羽, Han Xin 韩信, and many commanders from both the Nationalist and the Communist parties in China's modern history, were born in this area. The high number of military talents tells something about the nature of the people in northern Jiāngsū. With less favored nature, northerners often grow up to be very independent, straightforward and direct.

Common Surnames in Jiangsu

吴 Wú — Location: mostly in Sūzhōu 苏州 and Wúxī 无锡. Descendants of Tài Bó 泰伯, founder of the Gōuwú 勾吴 Kingdom in the Shāng 商 Dynasty

徐 Xú — Location: mostly in Sìhóng 泗洪 County in Sùqiān 宿迁. Descendants of Ruò Mù 若木, the king of Xú Kingdom during Xià Yǔ's 夏禹 Era

朱 Zhū — Location: mostly in Nánjīng 南京 and Xúzhōu 徐州. Descendants of Cáo Xié 曹挟, the lord of Zhū 邾 Kingdom during the Western Zhōu Dynasty

周 Zhōu — Location: mostly in Huán'ān 淮安. Descendants of King of Wǔ 武 in the Zhōu Dynasty

顾 Gù — Location: mostly in Kūnshān 昆山, Sūzhōu 苏州. Descendants of Gōu Jiàn 勾践, the king of Yuè 越 Kingdom.

陆 Lù — Location: mostly in Yánchéng 盐城. Descendants of Tián Tōng 田通, a son of King Xuān 宣 of State of Qí 齐 during the Spring and Autumn Period

龚 Gōng — Location: mostly in Tàicāng 太仓, Sūzhōu. Descendants of (1) Gònggōng 共工, a minister during Yáo's 尧 Era (2) Jī Hé 姬和, a royal family member of the Zhōu Dynasty

刘 Liú — Location: mostly in Xúzhōu 徐州. Descendants of (1) Emperor Yán 炎 (2) Emperor Chéng 成 during the Zhōu Dynasty

钱 Qián — Location: mostly in Wúxī 无锡. Descendants of legendary Péngzǔ 彭祖

秦 Qín — Location: mostly in Sūzhōu. Descendants of (1) Emperor Wén 文 during Zhōu Dynasty (2) royal members of the Qín Dynasty

贺 Hè — Location: mostly in Zhènjiāng 镇江. Descendants of Qí Huánggōng 齐桓公 during the Spring and Autumn Period

范 Fàn — Location: mostly in Sūzhōu. Descendants of legendary Yáo 尧

The Grand Canal is still an important water route for transporting coal from north to south.

The Grand Canal

During the Suí 隋 Dynasty, Emperor Yáng Dì 炀帝, was accused of digging a canal that cost 3,000,000 lives and depleted the national treasury. This fact led to the downfall of the Suí Empire. However, today the canal is seen as important and culturally rich as the Great Wall, another Chinese legacy.

The Grand Canal or dà yùnhè 大运河 is the shortened name for the Běijīng 北京 – Hángzhōu 杭州 Grand Canal. The canal starts in Běijīng, China's capital, and runs 1,794 km southward to Hángzhōu 杭州, the capital of Zhèjiāng 浙江 Province. The largest artificial river in the world, the Grand Canal is 33 times the length of the Panama Canal and 16 times the length of the Suez Canal. It runs through six provinces and municipalities in China (Běijīng, Tiānjín 天津, Héběi 河北, Shāndōng 山东, Jiāngsū 江苏, and Zhèjiāng). The Grand Canal runs west-east, connecting five major rivers (the Hǎihé 海河, the Yellow River or Huánghé 黄河, the Huǎihé 淮河, the Yangtze River or Chángjiāng 长江, and the Qiántáng 钱塘 River). The canal historically served as the most important transportation passage between northern and southern China.

Part of the construction of the Grand Canal began in the Spring and Autumn Periods, when King Fūchài 夫差 ruled the State of Wú 吴 (mostly in today's Jiāngsū Province). Chinese rulers after Fūchài made efforts to construct other parts of the canal. However, it was during Suí Emperor Yáng Dì's time that the canal was extended and finally connected. A great facilitator of the transportation of grains, rice, salt, and coal, the Grand Canal contributed hugely to the economic prosperity and cultural developments, especially in eastern China.

Along the canal, there are more than 2,000 cities and towns, many of which are well-known water towns of China, including those in Jiāngsū (namely Sùqiān 宿迁, Huái'ān 淮安, Yángzhōu 扬州, Zhènjiāng 镇江, Wúxī 无锡, Chángzhōu 常州, and Sūzhōu 苏州). With two fifths of the Grand Canal running through Jiāngsū, the province's past glory and today's speedy development are much indebted to this man-made river which remains in use to this day in Jiāngsū.

The canal serving as backdrop for wedding photos

One big catch from the canal makes a fisherman's day.

The Grand Canal running through the picturesque city of Yangzhou

Provincial Heritage

The Written World

Contrary to their Western peers, scholars of ancient China highly criticized novels and did not even recognize the form as literature. Only poems and historical articles were considered worthy of a scholar's time and effort. Even the wild popularity of *A Dream of Red Mansion* or Hónglóumèng 红楼梦 and *Journey to the West* or Xīyóujì 西游记, two widely respected historical works of fiction, did not result in the formal acceptance of the novel as literature. It was only after the May Fourth Movement (a historical movement, dominated by "new thought" and "new literature," named after the date of a massive student protest in Tiān'ānmēn 天安门 Square on May 4, 1919) that novels gained favor in the literary and scholarly community.

Sun Wukong, a popular character in Peking Opera

JOURNEY TO THE WEST

The fictional adventures of a Buddhist monk and his three protectors have left a lasting imprint in Chinese folklore. The triumphs and tribulations of *Journey to the West* are based on the real Buddhist monk Xuánzàng's 玄奘 (the novel's hero shares the same name) pilgrimage to India during the Táng 唐 Dynasty (618 - 907 C.E.). Dismayed by the quality of Chinese translations of Buddhist scriptures, Xuánzàng left Cháng'ān 长安 (then capital of China, today's Xī'ān 西安) in 629 C.E. Aided by sympathetic Buddhists, he traveled across China, then crossed present-day Kyrgyzstan, Uzbekistan, and Afghanistan, reaching India in 630 C.E. The Buddhist monk stayed in India for 13 years, visiting pilgrimage sites and studying at the ancient university at Nalanda.

Journey to the West was published sometime in the 1590s. For its profound and enduring influence in classical fiction, it is marked as one of the Four Great Classical Novels of Chinese literature, the other three being *Romance of the Three Kingdoms* or Sānguó Yǎnyì 三国演义 (14th century), *Water Margin* or Shuǐhǔzhuàn 水浒传 (14th century) and *A Dream of Red Mansions* (18th century).

The novel's story is widely accepted as an allegory — the group's journey to India being symbolic of the individual's journey to enlightenment. Some scholars believe the book satirizes the Chinese government at the time. But perhaps the biggest legacy of *Journey to the West* is its characters, of which the Monkey King or Sūnwùkōng 孙悟空 is arguably the most popular.

For centuries, Sun Wukong or the Monkey King is loved for his intelligence, immense strength, and rebellious spirit.

Since its publication, "Journey to the West" has continuously given the Chinese artistic inspiration. The story exists in so many art forms. It was dramatized in the popular 1985 TV series by the same title.

Jiangsu

Sun Wukong, the snowman

Sūnwùkōng, a monkey born from a stone (translations refer to him simply as "monkey"), is the first of the disciples sent to the fictional Xuánzàng by the Bodhisattva Guānyīn 观音. Sūnwùkōng learns the art of Dào 道 (the secrets of immortality), and eventually comes to be known as Qítiān Dàshèng 齐天大圣, the "Great Sage Equal to Heaven." He is the most intelligent of the Buddhist monk's three disciples and protectors, but is also the most violent. Xuánzàng controls him via a magic gold band on his head, which causes Sūnwùkōng extreme pain when the monk utters certain words. Sūnwùkōng eventually rebels against Heaven, and his excessive arrogance proves to be his downfall when Buddha traps him under a mountain for 500 years. Scores of animated films, television shows, and comics featuring Sūnwùkōng remain popular in China, as well as Japan and Korea.

"Uproar in Heaven," a Chinese cartoon animated between 1961 and 1964, is still loved by kids today.

The love story between Jia Baoyu and Lin Daiyu, two main characters in "A Dream of Red Mansions" has won the hearts of the Chinese since the novel's publication in the Qing Dynasty (1616 - 1911). Released in 1987, the TV series based on the novel was an immediate success.

A Dream of Red Mansions

A Dream of Red Mansions or Hónglóumèng 红楼梦 is widely accepted as a semi-autobiographical work mirroring the rise and fall of author Cáo Xuěqín's 曹雪芹 family. The novel is instantly recognizable as a definitive work of Chinese literature. Written in vernacular Chinese, as opposed to classical Chinese, *A Dream of Red Mansions* pioneered the legitimacy of vernacular idiom.

The iconic work of fiction is not for the faint of heart. It is a staggering 120 chapters long and presents 20-30 main characters, framed by a further 400 minor ones.

The story revolves around a powerful family highly favored by the emperor. "Jiǎ 贾," the family's surname, has the same pronunciation in Mandarin as "Jiǎ 假" the Chinese character for fake or deceitful. The suggestion is that the family is both real and fictitious, a reflection of Cáo Xuěqín's real family and a fabricated story produced for literary consumption. The novel follows the episodic journey of the extended Jiǎ clan, made up of two branches, the Níngguó 宁国 and Róngguó 荣国 Houses.

Jiǎ Bǎoyù 贾宝玉, the heir to the Níngguó 宁国 fortune, is the central character of the novel. He is born with a jade stone in his mouth, a symbol that links his character to Daoist and Buddhist mysticism: legend dictates that a sentient Stone, abandoned by the goddess Nǔwā 女娲, enters the mortal world after begging a Daoist priest and Buddhist monk to bring it there. Much to his father's dismay, Bǎoyù 宝玉 prefers literature to philosophy, hates the morally corrupt bureaucrats that frequent his family's home, and is a sympathizer of

Cao Xueqin's former residence in a western suburb of Beijing

29

A book illustration by Chinese artist Dai Dunbang of young ladies amusing themselves with a poetry competition around Mid-Autumn Festival. Unlike most women who were illiterate, the female characters in the novel are educated.

Wú Chéng'en 吴承恩 (1500 - 1582)

From: Huái'ān 淮安, Jiāngsū 江苏 Province
Known For: Penned the novel *Journey to the West*

Born to merchant parents, Wú Chéng'ēn 吴承恩 received a traditional Confucian education in his childhood and youth and later became distinguished because of his clever composition of poetry and prose. But during his life, his name wasn't associated with the author of *Journey to the West*. It was only in 1923, when the prominent scholar Hú Shì 胡适 identified Wú Chéng'ēn as the novel's author that the Jiāngsū writer emerged as a celebrity of Chinese literature. However, doubts about Chéng'ēn's penning the iconic work of fiction have remained ever since Hú Shì made his acclaim.

Cáo Xuěqín 曹雪芹 (1715 - 1763)

AKA: T'sao Hsueh Ch'in, Cáo Zhān 曹沾
From: Nánjīng 南京, Jiāngsū 江苏 Province
Known For: Authoring *A Dream of the Red Mansions* (AKA *Dream of the Red Chamber* and *The Story of the Stone*)

Cáo Xuěqín was born into wealth and privilege. For many generations, the Cáo 曹 family were servants of the Manchurian Qīng emperors. Cáo Xuěqín's grandfather, Cáo Yín 曹寅, was Emperor Kāngxī's 康熙 playmate. It was under Cáo Yín that the family reached the pinnacle of its power and wealth. By the early 1700s, the Cáo family had become so influential that they hosted Kāngxī four times on his six separate trips to Nánjīng. But following Kāngxī's death in 1722, the family suffered an incredible reversal of fortune. Kāngxī's son, Emperor Yōngzhèng 雍正, was less tolerant of this Hàn Chinese family. He ordered the confiscation of the Cáo family's property and the clan was forced to relocate from Nánjīng to Běijīng 北京.

Little is known of Cáo Xuěqín's childhood, but it is certain that he enjoyed a life of privilege up until the Cāo clan's fall from imperial favor. Childhood happiness and affluence were followed by later years' hardship and poverty. Cáo Xuěqín passed away in 1763, leaving *A Dream of Red Mansions* incomplete. The novel is said to be a semi-biographical account of his clan's ups and downs.

women. He believes that "girls are in essence as pure as water, and men are in essence muddled as mud." The novel had a great impact on society's view of women. It encouraged the opinion that women should be elegant, sensitive, and delicate.

The novel, as can be expected given the Cáo 曹 clan's downfall, ends in tragedy. Although Cáo Xuěqín did not pen the final chapters himself, the foreshadowing in those chapters he did write indicate that the Jiǎ family's fate was not to be a happy one. Some scholars believe that Cáo Xuěqín's notes indicate an even starker ending than the current one, but writers Chéng Wěiyuán 程伟元 (circa 1745 - 1818) and Gāo È 高鹗 (circa 1738 - 1815) made the politically prudent decision to tone down an ending that may have been perceived as criticism of the family's harsh treatment by the emperor.

"Red Mansion" was a common expression referring to the living chambers of the daughters of wealthy families. The title of the book can thus be interpreted as "*A Dream of (Young) Women.*" The title and themes of *A Dream of Red Mansions* also coincide with Buddhist and Daoist beliefs that enlightenment is achieved only when one realizes that the world is simply a dream from which one must awaken.

Yang Xianyi and Gladys Yang

Frankly speaking, the popularity of *A Dream of Red Mansions* in the West has much to do with the quality translation done by a couple who spent most of their lives rendering many Chinese classics into the English language.

The husband, Yáng Xiànyì (杨宪益, born 1915 in Tiānjīn 天津), came from a wealthy banker's family and studied Western classics at Oxford, where he met and married Gladys Taylor (later known as Gladys Yang, born in China, 1919 - 1999). She was Oxford's first Chinese language graduate. Since they returned to China in 1940, the couple took on a huge project of translating Chinese classics into English. A lover of Chinese classics, Yáng Xiànyì did the oral interpretation while the wife dictated and polished the English text. After Communist China was founded in 1949, the couple worked mainly for the Foreign Languages Press, the largest state-owned foreign languages publishing company. On top of their Chinese-to-English list are some of the most well-known classical novels including *A Dream of Red Mansions*, *The Scholars*, and *Mr. Decadent: Notes Taken in an Outing* and poems of the Táng 唐 and Sòng 宋 dynasties. The couple's introduction of Lǔ Xùn's (鲁迅, 1881 - 1936) works to the English-speaking readership is also considered noteworthy and important.

Pearl S. Buck and Her Chinese Attachment

Pearl S. Buck with a Welcome House child in the 1960s. Welcome House was the first organization to arrange adoptions of Asian children to the USA.

Pearl (left) with her missionary parents Absalom and Carie, and younger sisiter Grace in 1901. Behind them stands Wang, the girls' Chinese governess.

Born to Presbyterian missionary parents in 1892, Pearl S. Buck moved from Hillsboro, West Virginia, to Zhènjiāng 镇江, Jiāngsū 江苏 Province when she was only five months old. There, she spent her happy days until the age of 18, when she returned to the US to enter Randolph-Macon Woman's College in Virginia. Throughout her life, Buck was strongly attached to the picturesque city of Zhènjiāng. She used to have Chinese people all around her. Her nanny was Chinese and so were her private Chinese culture instructor and best friends. Before Buck learned English from her mother and tutor, Chinese was her first language. Without the language barrier, she was able to know many wonderful, culturally-related stories and understand the lives of Chinese people.

Throughout the first half of a long and prolific life as an author, Buck stayed mostly in China, teaching, writing, and mothering, with only some short intervals to go back to the US, either to pursue graduate studies at Cornell University, or to visit her parents. In 1930, she published her first novel, *East Wind, West Wind*. For a time, she and her husband John Lossing Buck, an American agricultural specialist, lived in a small city called Sùzhōu 宿州 in Ānhuī 安徽 Province. Buck's well-acclaimed novels *The Good Earth* (1931) and *Sons* (1932) were based on her rich experience of the region, and together with *A House Divided* (1935), they formed a trilogy that earned Buck several literary awards including the Pulitzer Prize and the William Dean Howells Medal.

Buck's other well-known China-related works are *The First Wife and Other Stories* (1933), *All Men are Brothers* (translation of the Chinese classical novel Shuǐhǔzhuàn 水浒传, 1933), *The Mother* (1934), and *This Proud Heart* (1938). "For her rich and truly epic descriptions of peasant life in China and for her biographical masterpieces," she, in 1938, became the first American woman to be awarded the Nobel Prize for literature. Her award is followed by a list of over 100 books of novels (many written using a male pseudonym), short stories, fiction, children's stories, and biographies, mostly China-related.

Buck lived in Bucks County, Pennsylvania, with her second husband and publisher, Richard Walsh, until her death in 1973, unfolding a highly accomplished life devoted to writing, charitable work, and fight to "eliminate injustices and prejudices suffered by children." Her US home remains a museum today. Among the several welfare organizations established by Buck, the Welcome House was the world's first adoption agency for Asian children adopted by Americans. In its five decades' operation, Welcome House placed more than 5,000 Asian children in a new home. Buck herself adopted several children and raised them in the US.

Today, apart from the literary accomplishment, Pearl Buck is remembered for her humanitarian endeavors in dealing with issues like women's rights, multi-culturalism, adoption, and poverty in less developed countries. And to most Chinese, Buck's Chinese name, Sài Zhēnzhū 赛珍珠 (taken from her middle name Sydenstricker) will shine for many generations to come.

Photograph of Zhenjiang before 1949. The charming city gave Pearl Buck so many happy childhood and teenage memories.

Pearl Buck liked to wander in the labyrinth of Zhenjiang's Songjie, an old district known for its Song-era architecture.

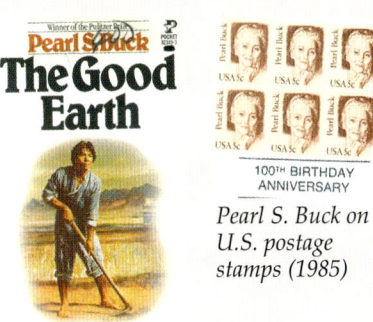

Pearl S. Buck on U.S. postage stamps (1985)

"The Good Earth," a novel by Pearl, is still on the reading list of American highschool students.

A painting by Shen Zhou. Representative of the Wu School, Shen Zhou was one of the first Chinese professional artists. He devoted his whole life to painting, literature, and calligraphy. His paintings were among the most sought-after art collectables of his time.

"Lady With Peony Flowers" by Tang Yin. Though known for his vivid portraits of young women and a Chinese "Casanova" in popular culture, Tang Yin was actually a talented but tragic figure, unconventional to his times, when most Chinese educated people followed the path of taking imperial exams to become officials.

Fine Art

Wú 吴 Culture developed in the southern part of present-day Jiāngsū 江苏 Province over 3,000 years ago. Yielding the throne to his young brother Jìlì 季历, Tàibó 泰伯 traveled south and established the State of Gōuwú 勾吴 during the Shāng Dynasty (1600 - 1046 B.C.E.). Tàibó advocated a mixture of central and southern Chinese culture, which in turn, became the Wú Culture.

In terms of location, the Wú Culture could do no better. Situated in the fertile basin of the Yangtze River, the Wú Culture was perfectly poised to reap the benefits of abundant crops. Meanwhile, eager citizens were quick to contribute to the economy and culture. Men distinguished themselves as masters of their trade, and the Wú Culture grew in fame and reputation.

THE FOUR GREAT MASTERS OF THE MING DYNASTY

Wúmén 吴门 (present-day Sūzhōu 苏州) was a cosmopolitan gathering place for intellectuals and well-known painters during the Míng 明 Dynasty (1368 - 1644). Records indicate that roughly 150 painters — about one-fifth of all of China's painters at that time — were in Sūzhōu. They formed an influential school of painting, the Wúmén School of Painting. Shén Zhōu 沈周

Life in the affluent city of Suzhou is reflected in the works of Qiu Ying. He draws happily the images of rocks, bamboo, and young ladies.

(1427 - 1509) was its most influential member, followed closely by Wén Zhēngmíng 文徵明 (1470 - 1559), Táng Yín 唐寅 (Táng Bóhǔ 唐伯虎, 1470 - 1523) and Qiú Yīng 仇英 (circa 1509 - circa 1552).

Shěn Zhōu was the patriarch of the Wú School of Painting. He was born into a wealthy, intellectual family and received a sound education. For his artistic work, he drew upon the painting traditions of the previous Sòng 宋 and Yuán 元 dynasties. He and his preeminent follower, Wén Zhēngmíng, exemplified Míng literati ideals: both shunned official careers and devoted themselves to self-cultivation through a lifetime spent reinterpreting the styles of Yuán 元 scholar-painters.

Táng Yín is Shěn Zhōu's student. He followed the traditions of the Southern Sòng Dynasty (1127 - 1279 C.E.). Unlike his teacher and Wén Zhēngmíng, he had an unrestrained personality and did not allow his painting style to be hampered by conventions. Like many before him, he inherited old traditions, but he is singled out as one of the Four Masters for creating his own style.

Qiú Yīng, meanwhile, was acknowledged for his versatility. Born into a peasant family, Qiú Yīng painted with support from wealthy patrons. He copied the work of early masters but incorporated many techniques and a varied palette to create his popular religious and landscape paintings.

THE EIGHT ECCENTRICS OF YANGZHOU

The Eight Eccentrics of Yángzhōu 扬州 or Yángzhōu Bāguài 扬州八怪 were a group of artists who shared common characteristics in their lives and art. Some scholars argue that the group was larger than their title indicates, but in general, eight artists are considered to form the group: Wāng Shìshèn 汪士慎, Huáng Shèn 黄慎, Jīn Nóng 金农, Gāo Xiáng 高翔, Lǐ Shàn 李鳝 (李鱓), Zhèng Xiè 郑燮, Lǐ Fāngyīng 李方膺 and Luó Pìn 罗聘.

Many of these artists were initially scholar-painters who pursued art in the literati tradition. They later became professional painters and flocked to Yángzhōu to sell their paintings and calligraphy to earn a better living.

Paintings by the Eight Eccentrics did not follow the old brushstroke conventions, making their artwork appear strange when compared with other paintings of the time. The artists shared similar life experiences, and they drew upon those experiences in their work. They were all born into poor yet intellectual families, served and resigned from (or never served) the Qīng 清 Dynasty (1616 - 1911), and all made their living by selling their paintings. The eccentrics looked down upon the corruption of Qīng officials and reflected their discontent in their paintings and calligraphy, which added a depth and meaning to their work.

Because they were in close contact with the lower rungs of society, the artists became preoccupied with the suffering of the people. Zhèng Xiè, who angered officials by opening a shelter for the poor, wrote on one of his bamboo paintings: "Listening to the waving bamboo lying in my office, I imagine it to be the complaints of the people; low is the rank of a county magistrate, I am concerned about every detail of my people."

The most favorite theme in Zheng Xie's (AKA Zheng Banqiao) paintings is the bamboo, symbolic of his unbending characters against a backdrop of corruption and moral decline in the Qing Dynasty.

Painting of orchids by Luo Pin, collected by the Nanjing Museum. Painting birds, flowers, rocks, and bamboo was Yangzhou Baguai's specialty. While doing so, the artists felt free in using freehand brushwork.

Modern Masters

The modern masters who are closely associated with the Wú culture are Xú Bēihóng 徐悲鸿 and Liú Hǎisù 刘海粟, two prominent artists from Jiāngsū Province. They were both educated first in China and then abroad. The study abroad had given them opportunities to combine Eastern and Western elements into their art creations.

Liu Haisu's works are known for his bold use of colors and the capacity to blend different art trends, Chinese and Western.

Painting of a galloping horse done with ink on paper by Xu Beihong. His horses are well-known for a nice combination of Western and traditional Chinese painting skills.

Rabindranath Tagore by Xu Beihong. A winner of 1913 Nobel Prize in Literature, Tagore (1861 - 1941) organized several of Xu Beihong's solo exhibitions in India during the 1930s.

"Foolish Man Moving Mountains," a signature piece by Xu Beihong. The theme was taken from a famous fable of an old man leading his whole family to level a mountain, supposedly blocking their way.

Xú Bēihóng 徐悲鸿 (1895 - 1953)

From: Yíxīng 宜兴 County, Jiāngsū
Known For: His contemporary painting style, a successful art educator

Xú Bēihóng began his artistic career at an early age. His father guided his calligraphy practice from the age of six, and then introduced him to Chinese painting at the age of nine.

He moved to Shànghǎi in 1915 and earned his living illustrating for publications and selling his own paintings. He later taught at Peking University's Art School. In 1919, he received a scholarship abroad and left Shànghǎi to study at Ecole Nationale Superieure des Beaux Arts in Paris.

Fusing the Western classical realist techniques he learned while abroad with his traditional Chinese skills, Xú Bēihóng created a new form of painting. He remains, however, best known for his traditional Chinese paintings of shuǐmòhuà 水墨画, or depictions of birds and horses.

Upon his return to China, Xú Bēihóng taught at several universities. In 1933, he organized an exhibition of modern Chinese paintings to tour Europe. During World War II, he traveled to Southeast Asia to hold exhibitions in Singapore and India. The proceeds from these exhibitions went to Chinese people suffering from the war.

After the founding of the People's Republic of China in 1949, Xú became president of the Central Academy of Fine Arts. He died of a stroke shortly afterwards in 1953.

Liú Hǎisù 刘海粟 (1896 - 1994)

From: Chángzhōu 常州, Jiāngsū
Known For: Being an artistic rebel and revolutionizing art education in China

Liú Hǎisù had a rebellious streak that eventually made him an artistic sensation. When he was 14, he traveled on his own to Shànghǎi 上海 to learn Western painting. The following year, he returned to Jiāngsū and set up a painting school, teaching and continuing to teach himself as well. In 1912, to escape an arranged marriage, Liú Hǎisù fled once more to Shànghǎi. He eventually established the Shànghǎi Art School with two other peers.

The school first introduced model painting, though at first only male models could be found. When an exhibition in 1917 included nude works, the school, and Liú Hǎisù, became embroiled in controversy. Rather than tone things down, he persevered. Soon the school had found its first female model, and the ensuing criticism and public reproach enticed Liú Hǎisù to write a public letter defending his artistic decisions. But the moral outcry proved too great, and the local government prohibited further use of nude models in the school in 1926.

Amidst the controversy surrounding his school, Liú Hǎisù still found time to maintain contact with his former teacher Cài Yuánpéi 蔡元培 (1868 - 1940), president of Peking University. He expressed a desire to paint in Běijīng. Liú was an advocate of painting on site; he broke the tradition of painting inside by bringing his students to the West Lake to paint in nature. In response, Cài Yuánpéi invited him to give a lecture at Peking University. In 1921, Liú Hǎisù made his inaugural visit to Běijīng, painting 36 pieces while in the capital. Cài Yuánpéi recognized Liú Hǎisù's talent and potential, even though China's art community remained wary of Liú Hǎisù's modern and impressionist technique. With Cài Yuánpéi's help, Liú Hǎisù traveled to Europe and spent two years studying masterpieces and acquainting himself with artists like Matisse and Picasso. He would later return to Europe as a teacher, rather than a pupil, giving a series of lectures introducing Chinese art to the West.

Throughout his entire life, Liú Hǎisù continued to influence art education in China. His teaching methods ran counter to the Chinese tradition of copying compositions and the techniques of old masters. He maintained that students should be given room to explore their natural talent while developing knowledge of formal art theory.

Liú Hǎisù passed away in 1994. His role as innovator, educator and champion of creativity has left an indelible footprint in the world of Chinese art.

Liu Haisu was an art rebel. In 1912, he opened Shanghai School of Fine Art, the first Chinese institution of art education, at the age of 17. In the 1930s, the school caused quite a stir when Liu Haisu started to use nude models in class curriculum, something considered unacceptable in a Confucian-based society.

Kunqu opera is considered the high-end of all Chinese operas, because most of its stories are romantic, the dialogue is poetical and refined. It is a drama form appreciated by the royal and the rich.

A book detailing the 600 years of the evolution of Kunqu opera

Kunqu Opera

Kūnqǔ 昆曲 opera is said to be the maternal form from which all opera in China has descended. Some scholars trace the opera's origins back to the Yuán 元 Dynasty (1206 - 1368), though it is more frequently acknowledged to have evolved during the Míng 明 Dynasty (1368 - 1644). Either way, Kūnqǔ Opera is one of China's earliest forms of drama and is still performed today.

The opera is named for its birthplace, Kūnshān 昆山, located near Sūzhōu 苏州, Jiāngsū 江苏 Province. It is characterized by clear recitation, correct pronunciation, and pure tones. Kūnqǔ combines song and complex choreographic techniques and symbolic gestures. During the Míng Dynasty, composers would score operas around tunes, with songs featuring seven or ten-character lines.

Kūnqǔ opera songs are accompanied by flutes or dízī 笛子, a small drum or gǔ 鼓, gongs or luó 锣 and cymbals or náo bó 铙钹, and the pípa 琵琶, all used to punctuate action and emotion on stage.

Tang Xianzu (1550 - 1616) was the most accomplished playwright of the Ming Dynasty. His achievements were unsurpassed for many generations.

In 2001, UNESCO identified Kūnqǔ opera as an oral and intangible heritage of humanity. The proclamation has helped revitalize the ancient art, which has suffered a gradual decline since the 18th century. The rigorous training and high level of technical knowledge required from audience members did not win over 21st century followers. UNESCO established a project to fund an annual Kūnqǔ Festival in Sūzhōu. The project also enables Kūnqǔ artists to offer training sessions, helping to generate awareness and interest.

Kunqu opera performed in a private landscape garden in Suzhou, Jiangsu. For rich Chinese families, such performances were put on for big occasions.

The Peony Pavilion

The Peony Pavilion or Mǔdāntíng 牡丹亭 is considered to be the highest achievement of Kūnqǔ 昆曲 opera. It was written by Tāng Xiǎnzǔ 汤显祖 in the 16th century and is one of a few dozen Kūnqǔ operas that continue to be performed today. The opera is often shown as a three-part series, unfolding over nine hours.

The Peony Pavilion tells the tale of Dù Lìniáng 杜丽娘. During a walk in the park, Lìniáng 丽娘 meets and falls in love with a young scholar. Alas, it is just a dream and she pines for him fervently in reality. She eventually falls mortally ill and on her deathbed, asks to be buried in the park where she met her imaginary love. Before she dies, she paints a self-portrait and hides it in the garden.

Time passes, and the audience meets Liǔ Mèngméi 柳梦梅, a struggling student on his way to the capital. By chance, he stumbles across Lìniáng's portrait and praises her beauty. Her spirit is awakened and she reveals herself to him, telling him that he is the one she has been waiting for, beckoning him to open her coffin. Liǔ Mèngméi obeys and Dù Lìniáng comes back to life.

The finale of *The Peony Pavilion* is often praised for its lively and humorous episodes. In it, we see Mèngméi 梦梅 succeed as a scholar, but not before he is punished for grave robbing. Lìniáng's stern father, meanwhile, does not at first accept the reawakened Lìniáng, but eventually admits that love can indeed conquer death.

Considered to be the highest achievement of Kunqu opera, "The Peony Pavilion", a moving love story by Tang Xianzu, is still performed today.

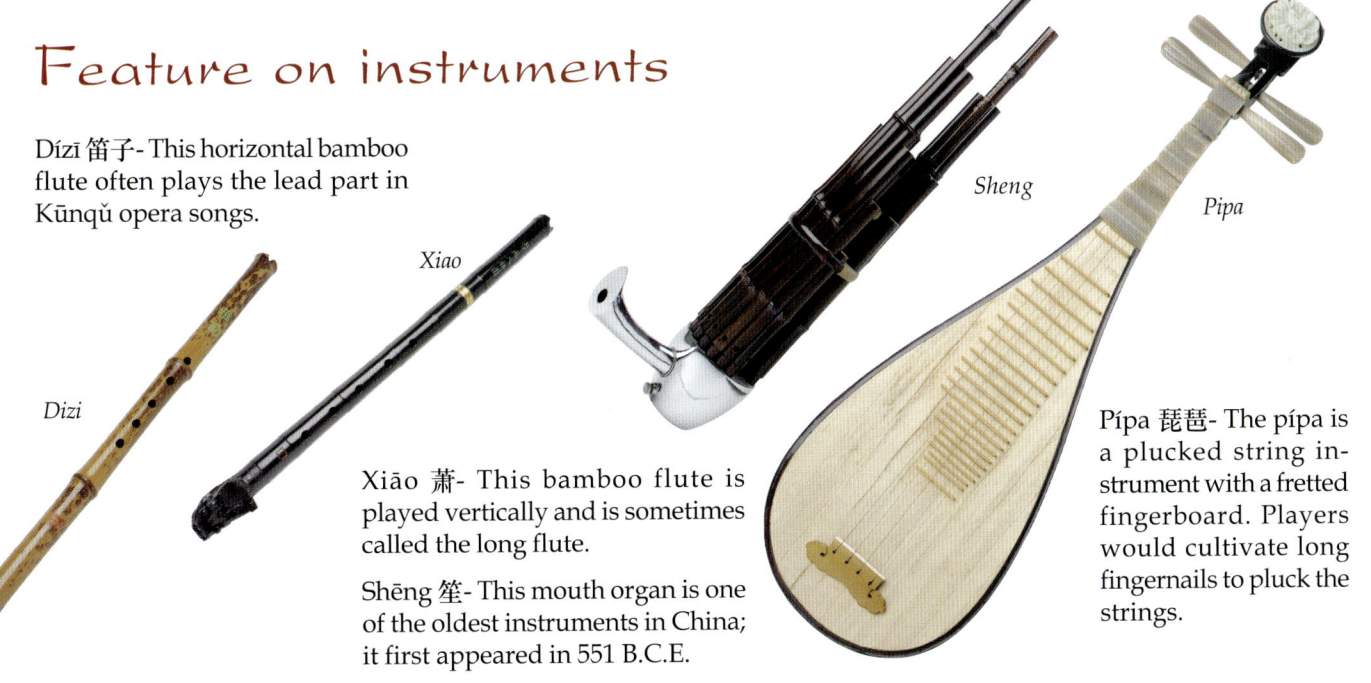

Feature on instruments

Dízī 笛子- This horizontal bamboo flute often plays the lead part in Kūnqǔ opera songs.

Dizi

Xiao

Sheng

Pipa

Xiāo 萧- This bamboo flute is played vertically and is sometimes called the long flute.

Shēng 笙- This mouth organ is one of the oldest instruments in China; it first appeared in 551 B.C.E.

Pípa 琵琶- The pípa is a plucked string instrument with a fretted fingerboard. Players would cultivate long fingernails to pluck the strings.

Science and Technology

The Daming Calendar

The Daming Calendar or Dàmíng Lì 大明历 was introduced in the fourth century. It was the first calendar to take cosmological cycles into consideration. Gifted mathematician/astronomer Zǔ Chōngzhī 祖冲之 recalculated the precession, or the movement of the earth's axis, on a large circle in relation to the star field and incorporated it into his calendar. The first measurement of precession had been made by the astronomer Yú Xǐ 虞喜 (281 - 356 C.E.) about a hundred years earlier. Yú Xǐ had measured it to be 1° every 50 years; Zǔ Chōngzhī's calculations indicated it was 1° every 45 years and 11 months. Today's measure is 1° each 71.6 years.

The calendar also included another measurement, one that remained quite accurate even today. Zǔ Chōngzhī measured the draconitic period (the time for the sun to complete one revolution with respect to the same lunar node) of the moon as 27.21223 days. Today's measurement is 27.21222. Using this number, Zǔ Chōngzhī was able to accurately predict four eclipses that occurred between 436 - 459 C. E.

Adopting a new calendar had huge implications for the emperor and his people. A calendar determined the schedule for daily life and ensured the dynasty was in sync with the heavens. Producing an accurate calendar was the highest achievement for an astronomer. Zǔ Chōngzhī presented his to Emperor Liú Jùn 刘骏 in 462 C.E. and invited other astronomers to comment. Dài Fǎxīng 戴法兴 (414 - 465 C.E.), an official favored by the emperor but not an astronomer himself, took up the debate. Dài Fǎxīng and Zǔ Chōngzhī argued over the merits of the Dàmíng Calendar versus those of the traditional one. Zǔ Chōngzhī lost the debate, mainly for political reasons; the ministers of the court sided with Dài Fǎxīng for political expediency. Emperor Liú Jùn later decided to implement the calendar but died before he could do so. Upheaval in the kingdom followed in the wake of the emperor's death, which made the introduction of a new calendar impossible.

Zǔ Chōngzhī died in 500 C.E., but his son continued to canvass for the implementation of the Dàmíng Calendar. The merits of the more accurate calendar were finally acknowledged, and it was officially accepted in 510 C.E.

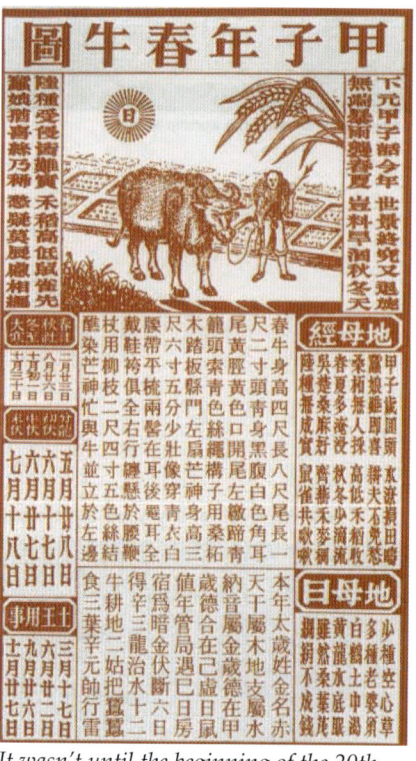

It wasn't until the beginning of the 20th century that China started to use the Gregorian calendar as is used throughout the globe today. Before then, daily life of the Chinese was guided by the lunar calendar. Even today, Chinese farmers still rely heavily on the lunar calendar system.

Zu Chongzhi built a boat that could travel 50 km in a day.

The Value of π

Several Chinese mathematicians contributed to the calculation of π. Zhāng Héng 张衡 (78 - 139 C.E.) estimated the value to be the square root of 10, or 3.1622. In 263 C.E., Liú Huī 刘徽, who was born during the Three Kingdoms Period (220 - 280 C. E.) calculated π to be 3.1416.

But it was Jiāngsū 江苏 resident Zǔ Chōngzhī, a mathematician from the Southern and Northern Dynasties (420 - 589 C. E.), who made the closest approximation. While at the Imperial Institute, Zǔ Chōngzhī uncovered several solutions, eventually settling on the value as being somewhere between 3.1415926 and 3.1415927. He used the fraction 355/113 and suggested a second fraction of 22/7 for rough approximations. His precise calculations remained unsurpassed until the 15th century, when Al'Kashi, a native of present-day Uzbekistan, calculated π using a similar method. Today the value of π can be calculated to millions of places. But to demonstrate Zǔ Chōngzhī's accuracy, uncovered during a time that predates not only calculators but also the abacus, π is shown here calculated out to 20 places: 3.14159265358979323846.

Geography: The Travels of Xu Xiake

The Travels of Xu Xiake or Xú Xiákè Yóujì 徐霞客游记 is a geographical

Xu Xiake discovered the Jinsha River was actually the northern section of the Yangtze River.

and topographical treatise that took the author over 30 years to complete. Born in present-day Jiāngsū during the late Míng 明 Dynasty (1368 - 1644), Xú Xiákè 徐霞客 (1586 - 1641) was destined for the imperial examination, having been educated in the ancient classics and learning to write the eight-part essay prescribed for the rigorous exam. But he refused to take part, and instead developed an interest in historical works, especially those documenting different places. Xú Xiákè eventually devoted the majority of his life to traveling throughout China.

He documented his wanderlust extensively. Records tell of his travels (often by foot) throughout the provinces of China. In them, he writes about locations of small gorges, the semi-tropical jungles of Guǎngxī 广西, and even the mountains of Tibet. There is a detailed study of the karst landform, noting directions, height, and depth. By traversing over the enormous bend and detour of the mountains in Southwest China, Xú Xiákè discovered that the Jīnshā River or Jīnshājiāng 金沙江, which many believed to be a separate entity, was actually the northern section of the Yangtze River.

A cover of the newly published "The Travels of Xu Xiake."

His discoveries were exhaustive. *The Travels of Xu Xiake* contains over 404,000 Chinese characters, a staggering feat for a single author of his time.

Xu Xiake made a detailed study of the karst landform.

Xu Xiake was born into a wealthy, intellectual family. His numerous travels in China were made possible because of his parents' generous support.

A Qing Dynasty edition of "The Travels of Xu Xiake."

Zǔ Chōngzhī 祖冲之 (425 - 500 C. E.)

From: Nánjīng 南京, Jiāngsū 江苏 Province
Known For: His mathematical genius

Zǔ Chōngzhī came of age at a time when China was making great advances in science, art and technology. The country was open to new ideas and possibilities. He was born into an intellectual family; his grandfather and father, an engineer and a technical consultant respectively, both served as officials during the Southern and Northern Dynasties (420 - 589 C.E.). Zǔ Chōngzhī received an excellent education from his father, was later sent to an academy under the emperor's patronage, and then proceeded to the Imperial Institute to study. Afterwards he was appointed to a position there.

During his lifetime, Zǔ Chōngzhī made several significant contributions to math, science, and astronomy. Arguably his greatest achievement was the creation of the Dàmíng 大明 Calendar, which took the precession of equinoxes into consideration for the first time. Other accomplishments include an accurate estimation of the value of π, the co-discovery (worked with his son) of the formula for computing the volume of a sphere, and a boat that could travel 100 lǐ 里 (1 lǐ = 0.5 km) in a day.

In recognition of Zǔ Chōngzhī's historical contributions to the circle and sphere, Crater Zǔ Chōngzhī (Crater Tsu Chung Chi), a lunar crater north of the moon's equator, and Planet Zǔ Chōngzhī are named in his honor.

Zu Chongzhi's calculations of π remained unsurpassed until the 15th century.

中国园林

Changing Landscapes with Every Step
Chinese Gardens

The gardens of Suzhou are actually a man-made landscape. Their designers have replicated all of nature's basic features in miniature on flat ground. Since it is impossible to move mountains, they built rock gardens. Since the course of rivers cannot be changed, they dug canals into the earth and made water flow through them.

Lu Wenfu, contemporary Chinese writer

The Chinese Garden

Traditional Chinese gardens are a national legacy. The most lavish gardens are found in the northern part of China, where emperors commissioned designers to construct vast mazes with lotus ponds, paths and walkways, bridges, and balconied pavilions. In the southern provinces, such as Jiāngsū 江苏, land was scarce. Moreover, the scholars and landowners that commissioned private gardens did not have imperial budgets to spend on them. As such, the architecture focused on creating the illusion of space, while ensuring an overall effect of simplicity and elegance.

Chinese gardens can be viewed as a backdrop for Chinese civilization. They served as meeting places for poets and painters and settings for peaceful contemplation. For a woman

The Ming Dynasty saw the influx of scholars and merchants in southern China who built themselves and their family members elegant gardens as seen in this painting by Ming Dynasty artist Wang Yun.

Chinese landscaped gardens used to be the mark of elevated social status.

with bound feet who could not walk far, a family's private garden may have been her only respite from duties and responsibilities. Rich men liked to show off their wealth by landscaping their property; a private Chinese garden was the mark of elevated social status.

THE PHILOSOPHY BEHIND CHINESE GARDENS

Daoism played an important role in the philosophy of traditional Chinese gardens. In the imperial and private parks of Europe, park designs reflected man's control over nature. Every tree and shrub was laid out to bring order and symmetry to nature. Hedges were trimmed and the landscape carefully manicured into straight lines and rectangles. Even water was controlled, such as in large reflective pools or as fountains. Traditional Chinese garden design, by comparison, was more irregular, even disorderly. Though Confucianism (which emphasized "the superior man") was the leading doctrine in ancient China, many people secretly believed in Daoism.

Daoism looked upon man as an inseparable part of nature. Followers believed in leaving things to their natural course. Chinese gardens, then, followed Daoist principles of harmony with nature: water flowed in every which direction, paths followed the lay of the land, and trees grew as if by chance. Though meticulously planned and executed, the finish of Chinese gardens look as if they were done capriciously.

Chinese families tended toward Daoist living by retreating from the outside world and enjoying their leisure.

Jì Chéng 计成 (1582 - circa 1642)

From: Sūzhōu 苏州, Jiāngsū 江苏
Known for: Being a highly-regarded landscape artist and garden architect

Jì Chéng made a name for himself designing several private gardens in Jiāngsū and other parts of southern China during the Míng 明 Dynasty. Jì Chéng and his contemporary Zhāng Lián 张涟 (1587 - 1673) are credited with the important change in direction in Chinese garden design that occurred in the early 17th century: from an elaborate, impressive style garden to a more understated, naturalistic one. The shift in style derived mainly from changing attitudes towards landscape painting. While very few of Jì Chéng's gardens remain, he managed to leave behind a literary legacy. He penned *Yuán Yě* 园冶 circa 1635, the first biographical study of garden design. In it, he advises designers that "The garden is created by the human hand, but should appear as if created by heaven." The manual remains an important reference for architectural and landscape scholars today.

Taihu rocks are common decorative pieces in Chinese gardens and thought to grant garden owners the sense of immortality.

Architectural Details

Architecture in all Chinese gardens is extremely metaphorical. As Meggie Keswick notes in her book *The Chinese Garden*:

Holes through a wall can be circular "moon gates," while sometimes they are in the shape of flowers, shells, gourds or vases. Balustrades can take on the pattern of "cracked ice," pathways can become "geese" and "meander like playing cats," pavilions over the water are "boats," and five pavilions set together become "the claws of the Imperial five-toed dragon." Keswick, p. 132.

Partially as a reaction to the embarrassing imperial extravagance, a taste for the "scholar's retreat" emerged. Such gardens were particularly popular in Sūzhōu 苏州, Jiāngsū 江苏 Province. Architecture for these private gardens may have been less extravagant, but it was still imbued with meaning.

Moon Gates

Even something as functional and prosaic as a wall had metaphorical meaning. Surrounding white walls topped with black tiles acted as dividers between urban life and the private space. Designers curved walls around the edges of the garden so the undulating tiles imitated a "flying dragon." Architects painted dividing walls a soft grey, wishing to create a subtle, unobtrusive effect. A circular hole cut into such a wall creates a beautiful effect on misty mornings or moonlit nights — the grey wall disappears into the shadows while the shape of the circle is cast on the ground before it.

Architects cut moon gates into walls to invite visitors to explore what lies beyond them.

These circular holes were known as "moon gates" or "yueliang men 月亮门." In China, the circle is a symbol of heaven, and it is also an emblem of perfection. Beyond conferring divine perfection, the moon gate also focuses the visitor's eye, forcing it to concentrate on the complicated patterns that lie beyond the gate.

Pavilions

Pavilions (tíng 亭) are another defining feature of gardens. They offer visitors a place to rest and direct the cultivated eye to specific views. They are also used as a place to read or as a stage for music performances. Similar to the tíng, the enclosed zhāi 斋, a small study, and the xiè 榭, an open pavilion attached to an entrance or jutting out to form an open gallery, are also common buildings in traditional gardens.

Exquisite pavilions are a defining feature of gardens. They are built for people to rest, socialize, and enjoy the view.

Rockery and Tai Hu Stones

In Chinese, landscape is shānshuǐ 山水, which literally means "mountains and water." The word invokes the concept of yīn 阴 and yáng 阳. Rough, still rock is juxtaposed by supple, flowing water. The former makes regular appearances in Chinese folklore, which is laden with magical descriptions of mountains. In ancient times, the prestige attributed to mountains was akin to worship. The Immortals, imbued with supernatural powers, were also thought to live in the mountains.

It should come as no surprise then that rocks, the elemental fragments that comprise mountains, hold significant meaning in China. Jiāngsū's Tài Hú 太湖 or Lake Tài 太 is famous for its limestone "tortured rocks." After being submerged in the lake for years, large rocks emerge strangely-shaped, both twisted and pock-marked. They have always been highly coveted as decorative pieces. They are thought to be powerful enough to grant garden owners the sense of immortality. In the past, emperors had them shipped to Běijīng. Transportation of the large and cumbersome boulders could clog vital shipping ports for weeks.

Flowers and Trees

China boasts an astonishing wealth of plant life. Flowers such as azalea, lotus, orchids, camellias, and rhododendron are common ornaments in private gardens.

Lotus

Lotus (héhuā 荷花) ponds are a luxurious feature of Chinese gardens. The large, water-loving plant affects a striking change in gardens between seasons. In spring and summer, the plants often completely cover the surface of a pond with their expansive leaves. In winter, the broken stems reflected in still waters mimic the strokes of fine calligraphy. Lotus flowers are much esteemed for their delicacy and pureness. Because of their close link with Buddhism and Daoism, they also represent heavenly mercy.

Lotus flowers are a must in Chinese gardens. They represent heavenly mercy in Buddhism and pureness in Daoism. They are also loved in gardens because of their striking change between seasons.

Orchids

Orchids (lánhuā 兰花) were prized by emperors and scholars alike. They were likened to the friendship of an honorable man. Like such a man's presence, the fragrance of an orchid would make an impression in a discreet and unobtrusive way, yet when it disappeared, its absence would be keenly felt. Orchids are also fussy plants. They require proper delicacy, but reward people with the patience for cultivation with their colorful and unusual beauty. Such qualities made these now quintessential Chinese flowers a favorite among the educated.

Orchids are favored by the educated Chinese. They are appreciated for their unobstrusiveness, representing the friendship of an honorable man.

Peony

The peony (mǔdān 牡丹) debuted in gardens relatively late, but quickly became a favorite. The delicate, blossoming flower came to symbolize wealth and rank, aristocracy, and beautiful women. The peony is believed to be one of the earliest flowers cultivated purely for ornamental reasons.

Fruit trees

Fruit (guǒ 果) trees added a colorful addition to ornamental flowers. Peach (táo 桃) trees, known as an ancient symbol of spring, marriage, and immortality, were often in Chinese gardens. Pears (lí 梨), whose trees were known to live for hundreds of years, signified longevity. In 1053 B.C.E., a duke sat beneath a pear tree to administer justice, and so the pear tree also became associated with good government.

Willow trees

Willow (liǔ 柳) trees were known for more salacious symbolism. In ancient times, Buddhists considered water sprinkled with a willow branch pure and hallowed. But the image of willow trees bending in the wind soon became associated with the waists of dancing girls, and from there it was a small jump to the suggestion of sexual freedom. The willow tree eventually symbolized singing girls and prostitutes. To respect female family members, men would not plant willow trees in the rear of their houses, where the women's quarters were.

Willow trees in the Zhuozhengyuan, Suzhou. The tree is often planted along river banks to accompany water's delicacy.

The Peony Pavilion in Hangzhou, Zhejiang Province. For the Chinese, the peony symbolizes wealth, rank, aristocracy, and beautiful women.

A painting of peonies and orchids by Empress Dowager Cixi (1835 - 1908) of the Qing Dynasty. Cixi was a powerful figure in modern Chinese history who is often held partly responsible for the downfall of the Qing Empire.

The Humble Administrator's Garden or Zhuozhengyuan in Suzhou, Jiangsu, is the quintessential example of a Chinese landscape garden.

A Walk through the Zhuozhengyuan

Emma's trip to Jiāngsū 江苏 Province wouldn't be complete without a trip to Sūzhōu 苏州. Sūzhōu is a historic water town dubbed the "Venice of the Orient" by Marco Polo back in the 13th century. Today, most visitors come to tour Sūzhōu's private gardens. Thought to be the quintessential example of a Chinese garden, they recently came under the protection of the United Nations Educational, Scientific and Cultural Organization (UNESCO).

Emma and her guide, Wú Gāng 吴刚 or Xiǎo Wú 小吴, decided to start their journey at The Humble Administrator's Garden or Zhuōzhèngyuán 拙政园, the largest one of the nine Chinese gardens protected by UNESCO. It was a busy day, with plenty of Chinese and foreign tourists milling around outside the entrance. The girls paid for their entrance tickets and walked through the main door to explore the 500-year-old garden.

"It's like a treasure box!" exclaimed Emma.

"A treasure box?" echoed Xiǎo Wú.

"Well, every time you think you have finished exploring, you go around a corner, and there's another section or a new space."

Chinese gardens are known for one specific feature – jiejing. It means borrowing views from far away. With jiejing, the limited space of a garden seems to be extended.

"That was exactly what the designer had in mind," said Xiǎo Wú. "This garden uses walls, bridges, and even trees to divide the space into separate and distinct areas. The architect also made use of a design technique known as jièjǐng 借景."

"What does jièjǐng mean?"

"It means borrowing a view from far away. Come over here." Xiǎo Wú pulls Emma to a pavilion and points to a pagoda in the far distance, beyond the boundaries of the garden.

"In this view, the architect is focusing the visitor's eye on that distant landmark. By doing so, he expands the limited space of the garden."

"So the garden doesn't feel small?"

"Exactly. This garden covers about five hectares. But using jièjǐng and dividing the garden into separate segments makes it feel much larger. Every door leads to another space and another vista."

"What about this here?" asked Emma, standing beside a hole cut into the wall of a pavilion.

"It's a window."

"But there's no glass. And why put a window here? Everything seems to be placed in this garden for a reason!"

"You're right. Let's go inside."

They walked into the pavilion to view the window from the other side. The rectangular window frames a large tree, bright green with spring leaves, and part of a rock formation.

"This was put here so visitors could see the beauty of the four seasons through the window, as if they were paintings. You'll also see many of these," Xiǎo Wú walked Emma to a nearby wall with an elaborate window styled in the shape of a flower. "They serve a similar purpose."

Emma and Xiǎo Wú continued their exploration. Ducking under a moon gate, they come to a section of the garden marked by a long, zigzag bridge.

"The bridge links the pools and islands," said Xiǎo Wú.

"This seems quite different from the bridges in town. In the city, aren't most of the bridges built in an arch over the waterways?"

"Right again, but this kind of bridge is not only for crossing water, it is also a way for the garden owner to show off a bit."

"How so?"

"Well, an arched bridge going straight across the water would take less time and material to build. But this zigzag pattern moves visitors in different directions so they can view the scenery from different angles. And it also shows that the garden owner can afford to build such a bridge!"

"Who was the original owner of this garden?"

"Wáng Xiànchén 王献臣, a former government official from the Míng 明 Dynasty (1616 - 1911). They say his original plan was to build a simple garden and live the life of a humble retired man, tending vegetables and planting trees."

"This garden seems anything but simple!"

"No kidding. Here, in the central part of the garden, you can see how the design is quite extravagant. Over a third of this section is made up of water, all of which had to be dug up. Many of these trees were imported from other parts of China."

Windows act like frames capturing seasonal beauty.

"It smells wonderful in here," said Emma, taking an appreciative whiff.

"Take a look at the name of the pavilion we're standing in," said Xiǎo Wú.

Emma read the stone sign: The Hall of Distant Fragrances.

"The Chinese characters are Yuǎnxiāng Táng 远香堂. This hall is named for the lotus pond we just passed. During the summer, the fragrance of the lotuses in bloom wafts into this room."

"Wow. And all this used to be for private visitors only?"

"A long time ago, yes! Private Chinese gardens were something only the wealthy and elite members of society could afford. But now it's a public space, open to anyone who wants to visit."

Lotus flowers, ponds, pavilions, Taihu Rocks, and willow trees are the essential components of a Chinese garden.

In Chinese gardens, bridges zigzag so that it affords people more time to linger to view the landscape.

Ups and Downs of Imperial Gardens

One of the few remaining imperial gardens, the Summer Palace in Beijing represents the Chinese way of landscaping, where cultural elements such as shanshui (mountains and water), tiandi (heaven and earth), and yin and yang are incorporated into the landscape.

So great and inevitable was the expense poured into imperial gardens that the rise and fall of an emperor's rule was said to be demonstrated in the escalation and eventual ruin of his garden. The quintessential example of a ruined garden marking the end of an emperor's reign is the destruction of Yuán Míng Yuán 圆明园 in 1860. Yuán Míng Yuán, or The Old Summer Palace, was looted and burned to the ground by a detachment of allied troops. Lord Elgin, a British Earl who ordered the demolition, had motives for doing so. The action was to retaliate aganist China after Chinese troops had tortured British prisoners in a horrific manner. Burning the gardens was Lord Elgin's way of striking the Emperor himself, the man ultimately responsible for the conduct of his troops, without harming innocent civilians. To the Chinese, the burning of Yuán Míng Yuán simply marked the downfall of the Qīng 清 Dynasty (1616 - 1911).

Cosmic influences played a role in the history of imperial Chinese gardens. Parks came to symbolize the strength of the empire. Emperors would use them as hunting grounds and stages for ceremonies and rituals. In time, emperors began incorporating legends of immortality into private pleasure grounds. Emperor Wǔ Dì 武帝 of the Hàn 汉 Dynasty (206 B.C.E. - 220 C.E.) attempted to lure gods to his garden by building replicas of the Immortals' homes. He duplicated the Island of the Immortals: two spacious lakes, three islands, and mountains. The emperor hoped the replica would be so enticing that the Immortals would mistake them for their true homes. Once there, they could perhaps be persuaded to share the secrets of longevity.

The Qing Emperor Kangxi built the Mountain Resort in Chengde, Hebei Province, another imperial garden. Jiejing, meaning borrowing views from far away, was also used in the design of the Mountain Resort, known as Bishu Shanzhuang.

Imperial gardens, naturally, were incredibly lavish. The strength and power of an emperor was unabashedly displayed in his landscaping. King Jié 桀 of the Xià 夏 Dynasty (circa 2070 - 1600 B.C.E.), for example, was said to have ponds of rice wine in his garden; Emperor Yáng Dì 炀帝 of the Suí Dynasty built a park 75 miles in circumference; Táng 唐 Dynasty (618 - 907 C.E.) Emperor Mínghuáng 明皇 had elaborate water and fan contraptions in his garden to cool himself during northern China's hot summers. Extravagant spending on private pleasure realms was a temptation too great for most emperors to resist. Some would order unusual flora and fauna such as peach trees or deer from other areas of China. Others fancied large ponds, filled with replicas of the Isles of the Immortals. Concerned about his lack of sons, Emperor Huīzōng 徽宗 of the Sòng 宋 Dynasty (1127 - 1279 C.E.) commissioned expensive fēng shuī 风水 masters to analyze the geomantic aspects of his imperial gardens. They diagnosed a flatness to the grounds, spurring Huīzōng to build a huge rock formation to concentrate the good forces in the landscape and block out the evil ones that were preventing the siring of an heir. He succeeded in fathering a son, but the expense of building the formation bankrupted the empire.

To the Chinese, the burning of Beijing's Yuan Ming Yuan in 1860 marked the downfall of the Qing Dynasty (1616 - 1911).

Master of the Nets Garden or Wangshiyuan, Suzhou, is a masterpiece of landscape compression.

Explore-A-Province in China®

Scenic Spots

Maoshan

Máoshān 茅山 or Máo 茅 Mountain in Zhènjiāng 镇江 has been an important destination for devout Daoists since the Hàn 汉 Dynasty (206 B.C.E - 220 C.E.). The mountain is home to several religious temples, as well as caves, natural ponds, and a surrounding forest. Compared to the scores of Buddhist temples, Daoist shrines are rare in China. As such, the Máoshān temples attract a large number of pilgrims each year. The hilly area also served as a base for national resistance forces during the Japanese invasion of the 1940s.

Tianmu Hu

Tiānmù Hú 天目湖 or Tiānmù 天目 Lake is situated in Chángzhōu 常州. Loosely translated, Tiānmù Hú means "lake of heavenly eyes." Its moniker stems from its shape: when viewed from above, Tiānmù Hú is said to resemble a pair of heavenly eyes. The lake is famous for its sweet water, which many believe is responsible for the surrounding area's renowned green tea. Several historic pavilions dating back to the Táng 唐 (618 - 907 C.E.) and Qīng 清 (1616 - 1911) dynasties round out the lake's attractions.

Langshan

Lángshān 狼山 or Wolf Mountain in Nántōng 南通 is a sacred Buddhist mountain on the flat flood plains along the Yangtze River Delta. Zhīyún Tǎ 支云塔 (Holding Up the Clouds Pagoda), a 15th century, five-story pagoda, denotes the mountain's summit, and the saffron-colored walls of Buddhist monasteries dot the mountain's forested slopes.

Hongze Hu

Hóngzé Hú 洪泽湖 or Hóngzé 洪泽 Lake lies in Sìhóng 泗洪 and Sùqiān

The Maoshan in Zhenjiang is a Daoist mountain shrine, attracting a large number of pilgrims each year.

Tianmu Lake is famous for its sweet water which is said to be responsible for the area's high quality green tea.

Wolf Mountain in Nantong is a sacred place for Buddhists.

宿迁 of the Huái 淮 River Valley, on the border between Jiāngsū and Ānhuī 安徽. It is currently the fourth largest freshwater lake in China, but was not always so vast. During the Táng (618 - 907 C.E.) and Sòng 宋 (960 - 1279 C.E.) dynasties, it was probably less than one third of its current size. When the Yellow River changed course in the 11th century, it forced the waters of Huái into the lake, which then swelled to its present size of 1,960 sq km (756.6 sq miles).

Qixiashan

One of the biggest attractions of Nánjīng is Qīxiáshān 栖霞山 or Qīxiá 栖霞 Mountain. Autumn is the best time to visit Qīxiáshān. It is during this period that the mountain is alight with the crimson red color of maple trees. Qīxiáshān is dotted with Buddhist statues carved into cliff-side caves and grottoes during the Sòng (960 - 1279 C.E.), Yuán 元 (1206 - 1368 C.E.), and Míng 明 (1368 - 1644) dynasties. There are over 500 Buddhist statues in total, ranging in height from a few inches high to dozens of meters tall.

Huaguoshan

In ancient times, Huāguǒshān 花果山 or Huāguǒ 花果 Mountain in Liányúngǎng 连云港 was believed to be the sacred residence of Daoist immortals. The mountain is certainly fit for an immortal. Huāguǒshān is almost entirely covered in a verdant forest and filled with fruits and flowers. Literally translated, its name is Flower and Fruit Mountain. Huāguǒshān was one of several mystical places visited by the fictional characters of *Journey to the West*.

Yancheng National Nature Reserve

A national nature reserve, the wetlands near the coastal city of Yánchéng 盐城 provide a haven for birds and other wild animals. It covers an area of 4,530 sq km (1,749 sq miles), and is home to 450 species of plants, 377 species of birds, 281 species of fish, 47 kinds of mammals, and 45 species of amphibians and reptiles. In winter, some two million birds fly over Yánchéng and one tenth of them make the reserve their home. Among them, the Red-crowned crane or dāndǐng hè 丹顶鹤 is the most famous. Six hundred out of 1,100 existing cranes live at the reserve through winter. South of the wetlands is the Dàfēng Mílù 大丰麋鹿 Nature Reserve. It was set up to protect the endangered Père David's Deer or Mílù 麋鹿, unique to China.

Dragon boat racing on the Hongze Lake

Because of its verdant forest filled with fruits and flowers, Huaguo Mountain was made into the home to the Monkey King in the "Journey to the West."

The Red-crowned crane is the most famous bird living on the vast wetlands in Yancheng.

Explore-A-Province in China®

太湖
Taihu

Jiangsu

Tàihú 太湖 or Lake Tài 太, literally "Great Lake," has bestowed its beauty and bounty for centuries upon the residents of the lower Yangtze River Delta. The third largest freshwater lake in China, Tàihú covers an area of 2,420 sq km and connects Jiāngsū 江苏 and Zhèjiāng 浙江 provinces, with 48 islets. It is also the source of a number of rivers including the Sūzhōu 苏州 Creek that run through Shànghǎi 上海.

Much of southern Jiāngsū's history is related to the Tàihú region, the birthplace of the Wú 吴 Culture. The Wú Kingdom was first established in today's Méi 梅 Village, Wúxī 无锡, during the Spring and Autumn Period (770 - 476 B.C.E.). In the 5th century B.C.E., Wú King Fūchāi 夫差 ordered a man-made canal dug to irrigate the vast land along the Yangtze River. This canal was later known as Hángōu 邗沟, and it connects the Yangtze and Huái 淮 rivers. Later in the Suí 隋 Dynasty, Emperor Yáng Dì 炀帝 extended this canal both southward and northward, making it the longest man-made canal (known as the Grand Canal) in the world.

The area around Tàihú has benefited greatly because of the water irrigation system. The region's agriculture, fishery, and silk production have made Jiāngsū a key player in Chinese history and economy. The cities of Sūzhōu 苏州, Wúxī, and Yíxīng 宜兴 were synonymous with the word "wealth" before 1949.

Tàihú's serene waters and surrounding misty mountains inspired Chinese poets and painters to pay homage to the lake time and time again. Tàihú's limestone formations, sometimes known as "tortured rocks" or "scholar's rocks," are coveted decorative pieces for traditional Chinese gardens. In recent years, Tàihú has suffered the tragic effects of Jiāngsū's thriving chemical industry; toxic cyanobacteria (pond scum) have turned the lake into a sickly fluorescent green. Jiāngsū plans to clean up the lake, and the Chinese government has shut down or given notice to shut down to over 1,300 nearby factories.

The deck built to welcome a Qing emperor was part of a private garden situated at Yangjiagang, Suzhou.

Buddhist sculptures at Wuxi

The ancient architecture in Luxiang Village by the Taihu is well-preserved.

Explore-A-Province in China®

Historic Places

Hanshan Temple

Hánshān 寒山 Temple in Sūzhōu 苏州 vaulted to fame after Táng 唐 Dynasty (618 - 907 C.E.) poet Zhāng Jì 张继 described the ringing of its midnight bells in the poem *A Night Mooring Near Maple Bridge*. The temple itself dates back to the Liáng 梁 Dynasty (502 - 557 C.E.) and is named after Hánshān 寒山, a famous monk that took charge of the temple in the following century. Though Hánshān Temple remains known for its melodic sounds, the bell described in Zhāng Jì's poem disappeared long ago. The current bell was built in 1904. Every Chinese New Year's Eve, it is rung to pray for happiness and safety in the coming New Year.

Zhouzhuang

Zhōuzhuāng 周庄 or Zhōu 周 Village is an old water town dotted with carefully-preserved ancient residences. Visitors are lured here by its antique charm, marked by strong local traditions and customs. Like its neighbor, Sūzhōu, Zhōu Zhuāng is often compared to Venice because of its myriad of canals and bridges. The area dates back to the Spring and Autumn Period (770 - 476 B.C.E), though most of the town's historic sites were built during the Míng 明 (1368 - 1644) and Qīng 清 (1616 - 1911) dynasties. The nearby towns of Mùdú 木渎, Tónglǐ 同里, and Lùzhí 用直 are also big draws to visitors.

Diaohua Lou

Built during the Qīng Dynasty, Diāohuā Lóu 雕花楼 is located in Guāngmíng 光明 Village, Dōngshān 东山 Town, in the distant suburbs of Sūzhōu. Diāohuā Lóu's name (roughly translated as the Building with Carved Patterns) is descriptive: the building is covered in gold, stone, wood, and brick carvings. Depictions of flowers, birds, animals, and historical stories are carved on the beams, pillars, doors, and even on individual steps. Not surprisingly, its former owner Jīn Xīzhí 金锡之 spent 187 kg or about 6597 oz of gold to build such a splendid three-story structure.

Han Dynasty Tomb and Terracotta Warriors at Lion Hill

There were 12 princes of the feudal state of Chǔ 楚 during the Hàn 汉 Dynasty (206 B.C.E - 220 C.E.). Most of their tombs are located in Xúzhōu 徐州. Noted among them is the tomb with terracotta warriors at Lion Hill. During the Hàn Dynasty, it was believed that one enjoyed the same lifestyle in the afterlife as they did while alive. As such, princes were buried with everything they would need to enjoy their new state of being, including an army. The terracotta warriors found in tombs are smaller than the famous life-size ones of Xī'ān 西安, Shaanxi Province. They were meant to guard the tomb of the king of Chǔ, a close relative of the founder of the Hàn Dynasty, Liú Bāng 刘邦.

Hanshan Temple is remembered by the Chinese for the bell-ringing from a Tang-era poem.

The picturesque water town of Zhouzhuang is often compared to Venice because of its myriad of canals and arched bridges.

54

Diaohua Lou, a building in Dongshan Town, Suzhou, is well-known for its surprisingly beautiful carvings.

Though smaller than the terracotta warriors in Xi'an, Shaanxi Province, the ones in Xuzhou are still worth seeing.

Slender West Lake is Yangzhou's most striking attraction.

The best time of the year to visit Slender West Lake is April when flowers are in full bloom.

Slender West Lake

Yángzhōu's 扬州 most striking attraction, Slender West Lake or Shòuxī Hú 瘦西湖, was once nothing more than a narrow river snaking through the northern part of the city. In the 18th century, Qīng 清 Emperor Qiánlóng 乾隆 expressed interest in a visit to central China. To impress and curry favor with the emperor, the wealthy salt merchants of Yángzhōu decided to build an unforgettable scenic attraction. They set about widening a long, narrow river, and decorating its banks with weeping willows, gardens, and pavilions.

Every effort was taken to ensure Emperor Qiánlóng was impressed, though several of the visiting imperials' observations had ironic implications for Yángzhōu's residents. As part of his visit, Qiánlóng was ushered to Diàoyú Tái 钓鱼台 (Fishing Platform) to try his hand at the local fishing. He was so gratified by his luck that he ordered additional stipends for the town. Local swimmers lurking in the lake, however, had augmented the Emperor's success by attaching fish to his hook. On another occasion, Qiánlóng made a passing comment that quickly stirred the locals into action. While touring the gardens surrounding the Slender West Lake, he was impressed by what he saw, but commented that he thought the gardens would be even more beautiful with a white pagoda like the one in his imperial garden in Běijīng 北京. The local salt merchants seized the opportunity as yet another way to please the Emperor, so they had workers construct a pagoda overnight. When Emperor Qiánlóng took a boat trip through the garden the next day, the merchants pointed out the outline of the shrine through the morning mist, much to his delight. Building something like this overnight was, of course, impossible in the 1700s. What the emperor had in fact seen was the body of a dome built from bags of salt hastily covered over in plaster. Once Emperor Qiánlóng had safely returned to Běijīng, the makeshift structure was replaced with a pagoda that still stands today.

The Grand Canal running through Huai'an

Explore Jiangsu Tours

Around Taihu

Sūzhōu 苏州 - Wúxī 无锡 - Yíxīng 宜兴 - Húzhōu 湖州 (in Zhèjiāng 浙江 Province)

Travel to southern Jiāngsū 江苏 to experience the core of the Wú culture. It is where you go to see ancient towns and traditional Chinese Gardens. The area houses the famous water towns of Lùzhí 甪直, Zhōuzhuāng 周庄, and Tónglǐ 同里. Don't hesitate to spend a few days in Sūzhōu, dubbed a "Paradise on Earth." Tàihú 太湖 close to Yuántóuzhū 鼋头渚 in Wúxī is also worthy a visit.

Suggested Timeline: 6 days

Along the Coastline

Liányúngǎng 连云港 - Yánchéng 盐城 - Rúgāo 如皋 - Nántōng 南通

Start your journey from the port city of Liányúngǎng with a good climb at Huāguǒshān 花果山 (mountain), the supposed birthplace of the Monkey King. The wetlands in Yánchéng are where you see the wilderness, a haven for birds and animals. On your way to Nántōng from Yánchéng, you can stop at Rúgāo. The small city awaits you to explore the secret to the locals' longevity. While in Nántōng, don't forget to taste some well-known fish dishes.

Suggested Timeline: 5 days

Along the Grand Canal

Xúzhōu 徐州 - Sùqiān 宿迁 - Huái'ān 淮安 - Yángzhōu 扬州 - Zhènjiāng 镇江 - Chángzhōu 常州 - Wúxī 无锡- Sūzhōu 苏州

The wonders of the Grand Canal can best be explored along this route that leads you to travel all the way from the northern Jiāngsū to its beautiful southern destinations like Sūzhōu. The many cities along the canal are witnesses to the provincial past glories. The Grand Canal route gives you a clear sense of what makes Jiāngsū as it stands today.

Xúzhōu is an ancient city, famous for the remains and relics from the Hàn 汉 Dynasty. The city of Sùqiān is a historic center for the liquor industry. By the Hóngzé 洪泽 Lake, China's fourth largest freshwater lake, sits Huái'ān. The city brings Zhōu Ēnlái 周恩来 (Chinese premier between 1949 and 1976) to Chinese people's minds, as it was home to him for 12 years. Yángzhōu, once a thriving city equally important as Sūzhōu, is in the center of Jiāngsū. Among its many attractions, the Slender West Lake is impressive with willow trees and arched bridges. Zhènjiāng was strategically positioned as a garrison to guard the entrance to the Yangtze River. American writer Pearl S. Buck (1892 - 1973) lived in the picturesque Zhènjiāng until the age of 18. The fragrant vinegar is something that you should try there. Máoshān 茅山 and Tiānmù 天目 mountains attract visitors to Chángzhōu. China Dinosaur Park is definitely worth another exploration.

Suggested Timeline: 12 days

Explore-A-Province in China®

The scaleless whitebait or silver fish is a delicacy popular in the Taihu region.

Sōngshǔ Guìyú 松鼠桂鱼

Local Flavors

Jiāngsū 江苏 province is home to Sū cài 苏菜 or Sū 苏 cuisine, one of the Eight Culinary Traditions of China. The terms Sū cài and Huáiyáng cài 淮扬菜 or Huáiyáng 淮扬 cuisine are often used interchangeably. The cooking style derives from the lower reaches of the Huái 淮 and Yangtze rivers. Given the close proximity to these bodies of water, fish and seafood play a prominent role in several Huáiyáng cài specialties.

The heavy use of seafood and protein led to Huáiyáng cài's reputation of being a cuisine for the nobles. It gained fame during the Suí 隋 (581 - 618 C.E.) and Táng (618 - 907 C.E.) dynasties, and was recognized as a distinct regional style during the Míng 明 (1368 - 1644) and Qīng 清 (1616 - 1911) dynasties. Huáiyáng cuisine reached its peak during the Qīng Dynasty when emperors Kāngxī 康熙 and Qiánlóng 乾隆 visited the Yangtze region, and local officials ensured complex dishes were prepared to please the imperials. Given today's increase in personal wealth and consumption, and the fact that Huáiyáng cài actually relies on quite basic ingredients, the cuisine is now accepted as one that caters to ordinary people. Being singled out by the Communist government may have also augmented the change in reputation. In 1949, Huáiyáng cài was the cuisine of choice for the first state banquet of the newly-founded People's Republic of China.

Typical Huáiyáng cuisine is known for its sweetness, and its frequent use of Zhènjiāng 镇江 vinegar, which is produced in the Zhènjiāng region. Huáiyáng chefs like to use delicate cooking methods to ensure a light, fresh flavor. Stewing, braising, roasting and simmering are the most common cooking methods.

Squirrel-shaped Fish

The dish, Squirrel-shaped Fish or Sōngshǔ Guìyú 松鼠桂鱼, is a work of art. Preparation involves deboning and meticulously scoring and carving a Mandarin fish (river carp). When it is deep-fried, the slices curl and unfold from the center, and the entire fish bends slightly. The resulting shape is meant to resemble a squirrel, with its head and tail soaring high. The crispy fish is served whole and topped with a reddish-brown sweet and sour sauce. The story behind the dish dates back to the Qīng 清 Dynasty. During a tour through the Yangtze River Delta, Emperor Qiánlóng saw a fish in a temple pond and ordered it to be cooked for him. To avoid punishment for killing a holy fish, the chef devised a way to "disguise" the fish as a squirrel. The emperor's appreciation of the crisp, tender meat and accompanying sweet and sour sauce was enough to elevate the status of the dish to national legend.

Yangzhou Fried Rice

Yángzhōu 扬州 fried rice or Yángzhōu Chǎofàn 扬州炒饭 is a popular dish and easy on most palettes, Western or otherwise. The essential ingredient is barbecued pork, which lends the dish its distinct, sweet flavor. Other ingredients vary, but typically Yángzhōu fried rice brings together shrimp, diced scallions (including the green ends), scrambled eggs, and cabbage. The origin of the dish remains a question. Some argue that "yángzhōu," similar in sound and pronunciation to the Jiāngsū city, is Hong Kong slang for

Yángzhōu Chǎofàn 扬州炒饭

barbeque pork, and hence the dish belongs to Hong Kong. Other accounts trace the fried rice back to the Suí Dynasty and Emperor Yáng Dì's 炀帝 favorite minister, Yáng Sù 杨素, whose love of the dish helped augment its popularity throughout Yángzhōu.

Farewell My Concubine

Farewell My Concubine or Bàwáng Bié Jī 霸王别姬 is a popular Xúzhōu 徐州 soup. The dramatic name suits the story behind this soup. "Bàwáng" 霸王 refers to an ancient hero, Xiàng Yǔ 项羽 (232-202 B.C.E.), while "Jī" 姬 refers to his wife Yú Jī 虞姬. "Bié" 别 means depart or leave. As legend goes, when Xiàng Yǔ lost his battle for the throne, Yú Jī chose death rather than enduring her husband's painful defeat. Xiàng Yǔ, in turn, so saddened by the loss of his wife, committed suicide shortly thereafter. The soup is prepared in a clay pot. Soft-shelled turtle or wángbā 王八 and chicken (pronounced as jī 鸡) are the main ingredients, with shallots, wine, and mushrooms added for flavor.

Nanjing Salted Dried Duck

For those who favor savory dishes, look no further than this Nánjīng 南京 specialty called Xiánshuǐ Yā 咸水鸭. The cooking method dates back over 600 years. The duck is first slathered in roasted salt, then steeped in brine, and finally baked dry in a covered pot for several hours. The end result sports cream-colored skin and tender red meat. The dish was created as a tribute to the royal palace during the Qīng Dynasty.

Triple Duck

The American cult dish "Turducken" may have found its match in Triple Duck or Sāntào Yā 三套鸭. This dish takes a pigeon, stuffs it into a wild duck, and then stuffs both into a fowl duck. When the meat medley is stewed, the varying textures create a sharp contrast: the fowl is tender, the wild duck is crispy, and the pigeon is delicate.

Bàwáng Bié Jī 霸王别姬

Xiánshuǐ Yā 咸水鸭

Suzhou Gourmet Foods

For Chinese people, both cooking and eating are considered an art form. This statement is especially true for those who live in Sūzhōu 苏州.

Aside from exquisite gardens, zigzagging canals, and arched bridges, the city's cuisine contributes to the legacy of Sūzhōu as a "Paradise on Earth." Situated in the heart of the "Land of Fish and Rice," Sūzhōu abounds in fresh water aquatic products, and seasonal vegetables. The plentitude of ingredients is a decisive factor in nurturing a fascinating culinary culture. Local residents love spending time planning what to cook, shopping, preparing, cooking, and enjoying food. Many of them keep the habit of taking well-prepared snacks between meals. Over time, they have developed a whole set of vegetarian dishes, famous throughout China.

People in Suzhou love eating a few xiaolongbao, a kind of stuffed dumplings, as a snack between meals.

Because of Sūzhōu's rich culinary culture, it's no wonder that people from other parts of China often relate the word "gourmet" with this fabulous city.

To get better ideas, one can read *The Gourmet and Other Stories of Modern China*, a collection of short stories by Lù Wénfū (1928 - 2005). By telling the story of a Sūzhōu gourmet's life, the author reflects with sorrow about the loss and fading away of Sūzhōu's post-1949 culinary arts.

The Suzhou cuisine contributes to the legacy of the city as a "Paradise on Earth."

59

Collector's Corner – Zisha Teapots

Serving tea to guests has been widely practiced in China for centuries. Chinese people not only offer good-quality tea to guests, but also pay special attention to teaware. They think that teawares reveal a person's status and taste. Among the top teawares, Zǐshā 紫砂 (Purple Sand) teapots or Zǐshāhú 紫砂壶 from Yíxīng 宜兴, Jiāngsū 江苏 Province, are perhaps the best-known and most valued.

Near the famous Tàihú 太湖 Lake, Yíxīng connects Jiāngsū, Zhèjiāng 浙江, and Ānhuī 安徽 provinces. It has been a historic center for pottery making. There, the earth is rich in iron and contains hematite, quartz and mica. After firing to as high as 1200℃, the clay turns out to be quite colorful — green, yellow, red, brown, but mostly purple. Early Zǐshā pottery varied in shape and function. Common people would use Zǐshā clay to make pots and jars. When tea-drinking became popular in the Táng and Sòng dynasties, Zǐshā was discovered to be an ideal container for hot tea, because it was both water-repellant and air-resistant. These two characteristics made the pottery stand out as a big purchase item on the list of Chinese businessmen. Thanks to the change of habit of tea preparation from boiling to brewing in the Míng 明 and Qīng 清 dynasties, the production and trade of Zǐshā teapots flourished in areas around Yíxīng. By that time, people found out that Zǐshā teapots were suitable for absorbing and keeping tea fragrances, and the Zǐshā teapots soon appeared in many households across China. Some were even shipped to western Asia and Europe via the Maritime Silk Road. The name "Zǐshā Teapot" became synonymous with fine teaware.

The uniqueness of Zǐshā teapots also lies in their design and production. Valued for their simplicity and elegance, they are a miniature synthesis of traditional Chinese art forms — poetry, painting, calligraphy, seal print, and sculptures. They reflect the aesthetic taste of both the maker and the owner. Zǐshā teapots by famous pottery makers have always been sought-after items and are usually worth the price of gold. Yíxīng Zǐshā teapots aficionados even include the famous Míng Emperors Zhèngdé 正德 and Wànlì 万历, and Qīng Emperor Qiánlóng 乾隆.

Today, true Yíxīng Zǐshā teapot collectors prefer to use one teapot for one kind of tea and are very particular about their maintenance. They believe the longer the pots are used, the more refined they become.

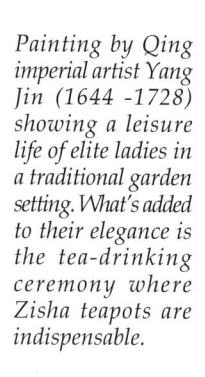

Painting by Qing imperial artist Yang Jin (1644 -1728) showing a leisure life of elite ladies in a traditional garden setting. What's added to their elegance is the tea-drinking ceremony where Zisha teapots are indispensable.

Zisha Teapot Q & A

How do I maintain a Zǐshā teapot?
Prior to using a Zǐshā 紫砂 teapot to brew tea, the teapot should be boiled for several hours in clean water. No chemicals should be used during regular cleaning.

Why do the prices of Zǐshā teapots vary so greatly?
They are varied according to the raw materials and techniques used to make them. Pure Zǐshā clay is usually porous and totally non-toxic, and thus costs more. The price is lower if non-Zǐshā clay is added. The value of Zǐshā teapots is also determined by the firing process and craftsmanship. For a signature piece by a well-known master, the price you pay could be sky-high.

Can I use Zǐshā for any tea?
Generally speaking, Zǐshā is suitable for any type of tea. But tea experts suggest that flat teapots best match Oolong tea because this kind of tea needs to be brewed at a high temperature. Thick and slim shape is suitable for Pǔ'ěr 普洱 tea and black tea. These two kinds of tea need a comparatively longer time to release the fragrance. Lastly, thin pots with big lids are best suited for green tea.

Suitable for absorbing and keeping tea fragrances, Zisha teapots are, generally speaking, fit for all kinds of tea.

Suzhou Embroidery

Jiāngsū 江苏 Province enjoys a long history of raising silkworms and silk production and is home to the famous Sūzhōu Embroidery or sūxiù 苏绣, popular in Sūzhōu 苏州, Nántōng 南通, Wúxī 无锡, Yángzhōu 扬州, Chángzhōu 常州, Sùqiān 宿迁, and Dōnghǎi 东海. With origins in Wú 吴 County, Sūzhōu, sūxiù can be traced back to as early as the Zhōu 周 Dynasty (1046 - 256 B.C.E.). Officials were asked to wear silk robes with specially designed patterns when offering sacrifices to Heaven. Embroidered military maps were used since the third century. Silk is considered one of the finest and richest fabrics to honor special occasions.

In the old times, girls in Jiāngsū needed to learn embroidery at a young age. For a Chinese woman, a set of skills known as nǚhōng 女红 that included needlework (mainly embroidery), weaving, cutting, and dyeing was the same in importance as reading and writing was for a man. In fact, a woman's embroidery capability was a decisive factor in her marriageability.

The art of Sūzhōu embroidery peaked in the Míng and Qīng dynasties because of Jiāngsū's thriving silk industry. The influence of Sūzhōu Embroidery reached through Jiāngsū, Zhèjiāng 浙江 provinces to far beyond. People took great pleasure in admiring its unmatched craftsmanship and aesthetic value - the exquisite needlework, sophisticated design and coloring. Today, the double-sided embroidery, typical of the Sūzhōu Style, is its highest achievement.

Unique to Sūzhōu Embroidery, double-sided pieces are knitted in the right angle without piercing the other side. In order to achieve this, threads are divided until they are almost invisible and joints are totally avoided. To create a design's vividness, many different colors of threads are used. Imagine stitching in 20 colors for just the eyes of a cat!

Today, in the small town called Zhènhú 镇湖, Sūzhōu, where Sūzhōu Embroidery first originated 3000 years ago, there are still 8,000 craftswomen practicing the supreme art of embroidery.

Today, many women in Suzhou are still masters of embroidery.

References

Books:

中华人民共和国行政区划简册，中国地图出版社，2007年
当代中国政府体制，陈尧，上海交通大学出版社，2005年
现代汉语词典，中国社会科学院语言研究所，2005年
走遍中国：江苏，平舒君，中国旅游出版社，2008年
趣闻江苏，肖飞、章晓历，旅游教育出版社，2007年
中国百家姓寻根游，《中国姓氏寻根游》编辑部，陕西师范大学出版社，2006年
中国历史秘闻轶事，张壮年，山东画报出版社，2002年

Goodrich, Luther Carrington. *Dictionary of Ming Biography, 1368-1644.* Columbia University Press, 1976.
Keswick, Meggie. *The Chinese Garden.* Harvard University Press, 2003.
Lou Qingxi. *Chinese Gardens,* Translated by Zhang Lei & Yu Hong. China International Press.

Websites:

The Central People's Government, www.gov.cn
Jiangsu Government, www.jiangsu.gov.cn
Jiangsu Tourism Administration, www.jstour.gov.cn
Suzhou Government, www.suzhou.gov.cn
China highlights, www.chinahighlights.com
Chinese folklore, www.chinesefolklore.com
Chinese culture, www.china.org.cn
China news, www.chinanews.com.cn & www.chinadaily.com
Chinese culture, www.chinaculture.org
Chinese heritage, www.unesco.org

Topical References

Provincial Overview:
Jiangsu, China, www.cbw.com/general/g11/g11.htm

Provincial Resources:
Nature note, www.yancheng.jiangsu.net/attraction

Provincial History:
Liu Bang, www.ask.reference.com/related/Liu+Bang?qsrc=2892&l=dir
Xiang Yu, kongming.net/novel/han/xiangyu.php
Li Yu, www.chinese-poems.com/yu.html
Zhou En'lai, www.answers.com/topic/zhou-enlai
Jiang Zemin, english.peopledaily.com.cn/data/people/jiangzemin.shtml
Hu Jintao, english.peopledaily.com.cn/data/people/hujintao.shtml

Provincial Socioeconomy:
www.guardian.co.uk/world/2005/may
www.time.com/time/world/article
Huaxi Village, english.peopledaily.com.cn/90002/95607/6524447.html & www.china.org.cn/english/China/155246.htm

Provincial Capital:
Nanjing, english.nanjing.gov.cn/
Yangzhou, yangzhou.jiangsu.net/
Suzhou, www.suzhou.gov.cn/english/
Wuxi, wuxi.jiangsu.net/
Xuzhou, xuzhou.jiangsu.net/
Lianyungang, www.lyg.gov.cn/template/lyggoven/english.html
Changzhou, changzhou.jiangsu.net/
Yancheng, yancheng.jiangsu.net/

Provincial People:
The Wu dialect, www.answers.com/topic/wu-dialect
The Grand Canal, www.chinaculture.org/gb/en

Provincial Heritage:
Wu Cheng'en, www.biography.com/search/article
www.britannica.com/eb/article
Cao Xueqin, renditions.org/renditions/authors
www.reference.com/search
www.web.uvic.ca/pacificasia/ChineseSite/hlm/author.html
A Dream of Red Mansions, www.reference.com/browse
Four Great Masters of Ming, www.wwar.com/masters
www.info.gov.hk/gia/general
Eight Eccentrics, www.home.seechina.com.cn/html
Xu Beihong, www.xubeihong.org
Daming Calendar, The Value of π, and Zu Chongzhi, www.chinaculture.org/gb/en_madeinchina

Special Feature:
Suzhou gardens, www.china.org.cn/english/e-sz/index.htm & www.ylj.suzhou.gov.cn/english/gardens.htm
Ji Cheng, www.gardenvisit.com/.../yuanye_chinese_garden_design_home

Provincial Highlights:
www.jstour.com
www.app1.chinadaily.com.cn/star
www.britannica.com/eb/article
www.vacationsinchina.com/Nanjing_attractions
www.travelchinaguide.com/attraction/henan/luoyang
www.travelchinaguide.com/attraction/jiangsu/suzhou/hanshan
www.chinareview.com/provinces/jiangsu/zhenjiang/index.html
www.seu.edu.cn/EC/english/jssz.htm
www.tipsofchina.com/w-chinatips/n1725.html
Local food, www.english.cri.cn
Jiangsu cuisine, www.travelchinaguide.com/intro/cuisine_drink
Zisha teapots, www.chinaflairtea.com/introteapots.html

The above websites listed as references were checked April, 2008 - June, 2009

Acknowledgements

Unless otherwise noted, all translations were done by Sherisse Pham, Sui Hong, and Megan Zaroda.

Unless otherwise noted in Picture Credits, all photos © Chinese Photo Gallery and © Phototime

Unless otherwise noted, all images © OCDF Publications Archives

Picture Credits

Cui Hongying 崔红英, Feng Renhua 冯仁华, Guo Wen 郭文, He Jinghua 贺敬华, Hu Xiaochun 胡晓春, Hu Zhilin 胡志林, Huang Renfei 黄任菲, Li Gen 李根, Lin Mo 林陌, Mu Jun 穆军, Pan Weijun 潘伟军, Peng Kai 彭凯, Ruan Zhong 阮忠, Sheng Qi 盛琦, Wang Kaicheng 王开成, Wang Mianli 王勉励, Wang Yunhong 王云洪, Xue Feng 薛峰, Xue Pengli 薛鹏里, Yang Bin 杨彬, Yin Ming 殷明, Zhang Bo 张波, Zhang Fanqin 张繁琴, Zhang Kaibin 张开彬, Zhang Qingzhong 张庆中,

Caoyuan 草原, Chengzhong 成中, Diyinpao 低音炮, Huiyan 慧眼, Jiayibing 甲乙丙, Jianghui 疆晖, Kuaile de Xiaoxiong 快乐的小熊, Liangyou 良友, Lvyouling 绿幽灵, Manmiao Dongfang 曼妙东方, Mujie 慕洁, Shanming 善铭, Taige 泰格, Tianying 天鹰, Yinyangyan 阴阳眼, Zhihua 止画

The impressive Zhonghua Gate in Nanjing was built under the orders of the first Ming Emperor Zhu Yuanzhang. Later, his son Zhu Di moved the capital to Beijing.

Silkworm Flower Ladies

Jiāngsū 江苏 and Zhèjiāng 浙江 provinces, are historically well-known for raising silkworms and silk production. In fact, in these provinces, sericulture is considered equal in importance to farming. When mulberry leaves turn green in May each year, many households in Jiāngsū are busy raising silkworms.

For many generations, raising silkworms has been seen as women's business. That's why a harvest of silkworm cocoons are called cánhuā 蚕花, literally meaning silkworm flowers, and women involved in the business are addressed as cánhuā gūniáng 蚕花姑娘 or silkworm flower ladies.

On Qīngmíng 清明 Festival (Grave Sweeping Day), which is around the 4th or the 5th of April, cánhuā gūniáng get up early in the morning, decorate their hair with flowers, and pray in temples. At monasteries, they buy more silk flowers and put them in a basket and offer it as a sacrifice to get rid of evil spirits that may harm a bumper harvest.

When they go home, silkworm flower ladies usually cook cánhuā jiǔ 蚕花酒 (jiǔ 酒 means liquor), a meal for the whole family. This celebration over dinner and drinking often lasts late into the evening and prepares the silkworm flower ladies to rise early the next morning to attend to silkworms.

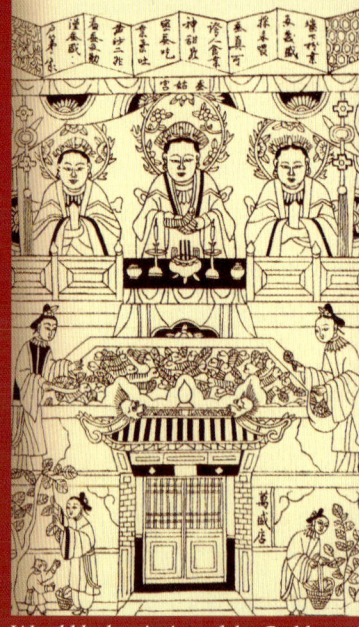

Old lady selling canhua, small flowers usually made of paper or silk.

Canhua ladies praying for a bumper harvest of silkworms at the Temple of the Goddess of Silkworms during the Qingming Festival

Wood block painting of the Goddess of Silkworms. She is commonly worshiped in southern Jiangsu and northern Zhejiang.

Old lady holding flowers. Women in the region often wear scarves wrapped around their head to protect themselves from the cool air in early mornings.